ENGINE HOUSES & TURNTABLES
ON CANADIAN RAILWAYS
1850 - 1950

ENGINE HOUSES & TURNTABLES
ON CANADIAN RAILWAYS
1850 - 1950

Edward Forbes Bush

THE BOSTON MILLS PRESS

Canadian Cataloguing in Publication Data

Bush, Edward F.
Engine houses and turntables on Canadian railways 1850–1950

Originally issued as a report for the Historic Sites and Monuments Board of Canada.
Includes bibliographical references and index.
ISBN 1-55046-002-1

1. Railroads – Canada – Roundhouses – History.
1. Railroads – Canada – Turn-tables – History.
1. Title.

NA6315.C3B8 1990   725'.33'0971   C91-093167-4

Based on a report (Microfiche
Report Series #209) prepared
by E.F. Bush for Parks Canada.

Published in Canada by:
THE BOSTON MILLS PRESS
132 Main Street
Erin, Ontario N0B 1T0
(519) 833-2407
Fax: (519) 833-2195

American Association
for State and Local History
Award of Merit

Winners of the
Heritage Canada
Communications Award

Designed by John Denison, Erin
Cover Design by Gill Stead, Guelph
Typography by Lexigraf, Tottenham
Printed by Ampersand, Guelph

The Publisher gratefully acknowledges the assistance of
the Canada Council and the Ontario Arts Council.

CONTENTS

ACKNOWLEDGEMENTS

The author wishes first to acknowledge the signal assistance rendered him by J. Norman Lowe, Canadian National Historical Officer and railway historian. Omer Lavallée, Canadian Pacific corporate archivist and railway historian, made a major contribution to the information contained herein. On the staff of the Public Archives of Canada, where most of the research was done, the author would cite in particular Glenn Wright and Lloyd Chisamore for their counsel and assistance with sources. Finally the author tenders his appreciation for assistance rendered by David J. Harris, Winnipeg, not only for his information on roundhouses in that neighbourhood, but for the hospitality which made the author's week there a memorable one.

Finally, the author's sometime supervisor and friend, Gordon Bennett, of Parks Canada, merits a citation for his meticulous attention to detail in the final stages of the work.

Be it noted that the whole of the text was written whilst the author was in the employ of Parks Canada.

Montreal CNR Turcot roundhouse, 1930s. — CNR Archives

INTRODUCTION

This book was initially written as a report to provide historical information for the Historic Sites and Monuments Board of Canada, which advises the Minister for the Department of the Environment on matters of national historic or architectural importance. The future of surviving roundhouses is precarious. This is a heritage issue of concern to those who are interested in the physical manifestations of the nation's industrial past, an aspect of Canadian history which the Parks Canada systems plan concluded was insufficiently represented in the existing system of national historic parks. While it is not the purpose of this book to comment upon the desirability, or the level, of commemoration of roundhouses, it should be noted that the Historic Sites and Monuments Board has deferred consideration of individual roundhouse structures because of the absence of information on the topic. The original report was therefore written to meet the basic reference requirements of the Board.

* * *

The traveller leaving a railway terminal or junction during the age of steam would probably have taken little notice of one of the low-lying, semi-circular structures depicted in these pages. Located in the yards, somewhat beyond the traveller's line of vision, the round-house was a vital part of railway operations, but one in which the average passenger could be expected to take little interest. The steam locomotive, of ever-increasing size, hauling luxurious name-trains, as well as the handsome neoclassic railway terminals, whose spacious concourses were thronged with passengers, captured the public imagination, and much has been written thereon. By contrast, even in the specialized literature of railway historians, the roundhouse and its attendant facilities, once found at every terminal and intermediate divisional point, have been all but ignored. Indeed, to the writer's knowledge, there are few English-language historical works on the role, architecture and operation of the roundhouse.

With the passing of steam power at mid-century on this continent, the roundhouse has fallen into gradual redundancy. With diesel-electric locomotives the roundhouse no longer serves a vital function. Diesels require much less maintenance, for which the roundhouse is not well designed. Engine shops of rectangular configuration serve better, although there are a number of roundhouses (67 according to present research, see Appendix A) still in service, used as diesel maintenance shops, and others again have been relegated by the railways to the role of storage depots. Inevitably, however, with the diminution of their function with the demise of the steam locomotive, a great many roundhouses, indeed by far the greater number, have been demolished.

Inasmuch as the roundhouse is a structure largely unfamiliar even to those who passed their active years in the steam era, the structure and function of the roundhouse are treated first in this book, in order to familiarize the reader with the subject. Then follows the evolution of the roundhouse over the course of the hundred years that the steam locomotive dominated the railway scene on this continent. Although the roundhouse and turntable formed an integral complex, roundhouses and turntables are treated separately in the interest of clarity, the latter forming the final chapter of the book.

CPR roundhouse, late 1880s. — CP Archives

Square House, Roundhouse

The roundhouse has so dominated the scene in North America that the term has become synonymous with engine or locomotive house. Nonetheless the roundhouse is but one of two designs comprising the genus engine house. Strictly speaking, neither design quite fits its designation. The square house is more often rectangular than square, and the roundhouse may more aptly be described as polygonal than round. Most Canadian roundhouses form a segment of a circle, and hence are fan-shaped rather than round. Writers such as Walter G. Berg and Marshall M. Kirkman used the term "square house" in distinction to the round-house, and this convention will be broadly followed in the succeeding pages, with recourse to the description "rectangular" house when this applies to a particular structure.

As with the story of Canadian railway technology in general, Canadian engine house development followed American development closely, after an early period of British influence. The predominance of the roundhouse itself is evidence of this, for in Great Britain the square house was preferred, although by no means exclusively, and European railways seem not to have been committed to either form.

It appears to be the case that American architects, railway associations and trade journals exercised an important influence on Canadian railroaders. Among the handful of writers who dealt with the subject were Walter G. Berg and Marshall M. Kirkman, whose *Science of Railways* (1900) in 12 volumes described the roundhouse as it had evolved to that time, detailing the desirable features. W.E. Dunham, mechanical engineer with the Chicago & North-Western, and Exum M. Haas of the Austin Company, Cleveland, were active proponents of roundhouse development in the early 1920s, along with Ernest Cordeal, who published a work entitled *Railroad Operation* in 1924. Bodies such as the American Railway Master Mechanics Association, the Western Society of Engineers, and the American Railway Engineering Association carried out symposiums and published papers relating to the most effective roundhouse and turntable design, and must be considered prime influences on engine house developments in Canada. A number of trade journals specializing in railway matters, such as the U.S. publications *Engineering News*, the *Railroad Gazette*, *Railway Master Mechanic*, *Railway Engineering and Maintenance*, and the Canadian publication *Railway and Shipping World* (after 1905, *Railway and Marine World*), provided a ready forum for improvement of the engine house, as well as descriptions of what had already been accomplished. Notwithstanding the fairly pervasive American influence, a note of Canadian individuality in the adaptation of structures to a severe climate might be anticipated, but in this respect the northern states were obviously subject to the same climate as the adjoining Canadian provinces. A high proportion of Canadian railways operated within 200 miles of the international boundary, hence climate did not play a major role in evolving a particularly Canadian style of architecture.

The square house, as it evolved in Britain and on the Continent, was of three basic types: the "run-through" design, open at both ends; the sub-track type, open at one end with buffers at the other; and the radial-track type, centred on one or more interior turntables. A number of early Canadian engine houses answered to one or another of these descriptions, although the roundhouse form, evolving at the same time, became predominant by the 1880s. These early Canadian square houses were on a very small scale, but early in the 20th century two very large square houses with interior turntables were built.

The roundhouse, by contrast, consisted of radiating stalls, forming a semicircular to circular pattern, whose tracks converged on a central turntable. Since the turntable was the *sine qua non* of the roundhouse, the entrance or front wall of the roundhouse faced the turntable; the back wall formed the circumference of the structure. The turntable, pivoting

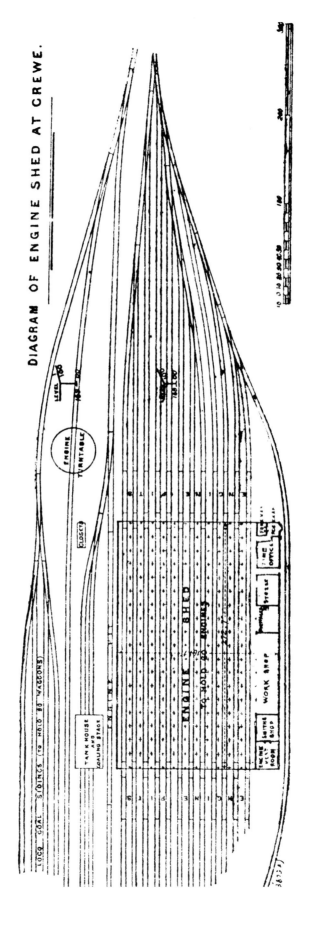

DIAGRAM OF ENGINE SHED AT CREWE.

Diagram of engine shed at Crewe. "Through and Through" (tracks in one end, out the other), built 1897, London & North Western R.R. In the U.K. this type of engine house was more common than the roundhouse.

— The Canadian Engineer, June 1897, Vol. 5, No. 2, p. 34

12

about a central bearing in a pit, was open to the elements as the roundhouse evolved in North America. Both forms of engine house offered advantages and limitations. The question arises as to why the roundhouse form predominated to the degree that it did in North America, and to this no satisfactory answer has yet been found. At the date of writing it is not known whether or not the roundhouse design originated in the United States. There was a roundhouse in Camden, England, as early as 1846, but research has yet to determine when and where the first roundhouse was built in the United States.[1]

Before discussion of the advantages and disadvantages of the two types of engine house, the reader is referred to plans of the respective layouts, which may serve to clarify what follows. Included as illustration is a diagram of a large "run-through" type of "square" house at Crewe, England, and the Canadian Pacific roundhouses and attendant facilities at Toronto.

A key factor in considering the merits of the square and the roundhouse is the facility with which locomotives can be turned and shifted from one part of the house to another. With a roundhouse a turntable is indispensable, to the degree that a breakdown of the turntable resulted in a blockade of the roundhouse. With the square house a transfer table, a device used for moving locomotives at right angles, could be used, or alternatively a wye track, a spur track leading to a dead end with two approach tracks leading in from opposite directions; by this means a locomotive could be run in and backed out, so reversing its direction, or backed into the wye and driven out by the other exit. A wye track layout took up considerable space. The turntable was a very costly piece of equipment, and the transfer table even more so. Obviously two key factors in considering the merits of the two types were cost and space.[2]

What were the merits of the square house, the preferred type in the United Kingdom? As expounded by the American publication *Engineering News,* whose editor believed the type merited more consideration that it had received from American railroaders, the square house was cheaper to build and less costly to maintain than the roundhouse. Also, the square, or rectangular house was simpler to extend for the accommodation of ever larger locomotives, a factor nowhere as urgent as in the United States, particularly after 1910, when locomotives of unprecedented size were being outshopped with increasing frequency. On the crucial issue of space, *Engineering News* estimated that the combination of a square house with a transfer table took up one quarter less space than a roundhouse with equivalent accommodation, but admitted that the transfer table was more expensive than the turntable, albeit without quoting any figures. Providing plenty of space was available, the square house might dispense with the transfer table altogether, utilizing instead a long track approach with ladder-track connection (in which a number of tracks lead into a single approach track) or a wye. This type of layout would be more economical than either the square house with transfer table or the roundhouse with turntable. It follows that where space was constricted, the choice lay between the square or rectangular house with a transfer table or the roundhouse with turntable. Yet another advantage offered by the square house was that it was, with fewer doors, easier to heat. In the roundhouse design there was, of necessity, a set of doors for each locomotive housed, and roundhouse swing doors were notoriously drafty. Notwithstanding the rigours of the Canadian climate, the advantages of the square house in this respect seem to have had little influence. Finally the square house, particularly the "run-through" type, was easier to evacuate in case of fire. Such advantages led the *Engineering News* editor to recommend the merits of the square house for further consideration. In spite of this recommendation, American railroad practice almost totally favoured the roundhouse design for the large engine houses,

---

1   Marcus Binney and David Pearce, ed., *Railway Architecture,* (London: Orbis Publishing, 1979), p. 161; *Historic American Engineering Record Catalog,* 1976, comp. Donald E. Sackhelm, (Washington, D.C., National Park Service, 1976), p. 171.
2   *Engineering News,* (New York: Hill Publishing), 5 Dec. 1912, p. 1066.

with the square or rectangular house occasionally resorted to for smaller structures. One reason adduced by the *Engineering News* for European reservations on the roundhouse design was military; in France and Germany the turntable was in disfavour because of the blockade and tie-up of locomotives in roundhouses in case of a malfunctioning turntable.[3]

Turning to the roundhouse, so much a feature of the North American scene, it is a little difficult to account for this strong preference dating back to the early days of railroading on this continent. That the roundhouse had advantages is indisputable, but the almost total preference shown by American railroad men for this design, at least for the larger engine houses, is less easy to explain. Walter Berg, writing in 1893, gave as reasons the economy of space offered by the roundhouse and the good natural light available from the spacious windows on the back or outside wall (locomotives were parked with the front end of the locomotive facing the back wall of the roundhouse). As well, roundhouse design, with its radiating stalls, afforded more space at the back to work on the front end of the locomotive, where much of the maintenance work involving the cylinders, valve gear, smoke box and boiler was called for. Roundhouses could be added on, stall by stall, until in some cases a full circle was formed, but the accommodation of bigger locomotives was less easily affected than with the square house; the roundhouse back wall had to be extended further out, which in fact was frequently done. Other roundhouses were simply rendered obsolete by the mammoth dimensions of the new locomotives and were replaced. The prime disadvantage of the roundhouse was evacuation in case of fire. The *News* editor cited an hour or more for the average roundhouse, compared with about ten minutes for a square house of equivalent size. Engine houses to accommodate 20 locomotives or more, however, called for a transfer table in the case of a square house, and the added cost of this over the turntable may well have been a factor in the American preference for the roundhouse. As Berg pointed out, risk of blockade was the Achilles heel of the roundhouse. The embarrassing accident depicted at Beaverton, Ontario, is a case in point. From time to time hostlers moving engines out of a roundhouse missed the turntable, putting the locomotive in the pit, a recurrent nightmare to every roundhouse foreman. Until the locomotive was lifted from the pit and the turntable restored to service, the roundhouse was blockaded. The structure of the roundhouse was more complicated and it was more expensive to build and maintain than was the simpler rectangular house, and the oversight of the work more difficult. Notwithstanding the obvious disadvantages, the roundhouse, for all but small structures, held the field in America, and in Canada only two large engine houses forsook the roundhouse design.[4]

Presumably, whether in Europe or North America, the earliest engine houses, designed to house one or two locomotives only, were simple rectangular sheds. With the proliferation of locomotives as the operation of each railway expanded, engine houses increased in size, and after the turn of the century to an increasing degree to accommodate locomotives of unprecedented size. Two trends were basic to engine houses everywhere: increased size and use of non-combustible construction material, resulting in the fireproof engine house by the 1930s.

Inasmuch as the roundhouse form so predominated in Canada, it is fitting that a preliminary study be made of the mature roundhouse as it had evolved by the early 20th century.

---

3   ibid. 24 Oct. 1912, pp. 785-6.
4   Walter G. Berg, *American Railroads*, (New York: John Wiley, 1893), pp. 166-7, 169, also 168; *Engineering News*, 5 Dec. 1912, p. 1066; Walter G. Berg, *Buildings and Structures of American Railroads*, No. 7 of series Train Shed Cyclopedia, (Novato, Cal: Newton K. Gregg, 1973), pp. 168-9, 167; Marcus Binney and David Pearce, op. cit., pp. 165, 167, 171.

Turntable pit mishap, Beaverton, Ontario, n.d.   – NAC

CPR yard layout, Toronto.

– *Canadian Railway & Marine World*, Dec. 1929, p. 740

THE ANATOMY OF A ROUNDHOUSE

The roundhouse was the central feature in a yard complex, which is well depicted by the CPR Toronto (John Street) roundhouse, built in 1929. To the north of the roundhouse are the passenger yards, where were parked cars not in use but available for road service. (Fifty years ago passenger yards were extensive, with several hundred cars standing in long lines on a score or more of tracks. Today passenger yards are a tithe of their former dimensions, reflecting the decimation of the passenger service.) Adjacent thereto, although not shown on this drawing, were the considerably more extensive freight yards, serving a similar function. Associated with the passenger yard were the car repair shops, with equivalent facilities for freight. On the approaches to the roundhouse and turn table were the ash pits, rectangular depressions between the tracks, over which the ashes from the locomotive fireboxes were drawn. Also on the approaches to the turntable were sooty, blackened structures, generally of frame construction and two or three storeys high. These were the coaling plant and the sandhouse (sand being dispensed from the locomotive's sand dome onto the track when needed to aid traction), from which the locomotive's tender and sand dome were filled by gravity flow from above. Incoming locomotives stopped over the ash pit, and outgoing locomotives stopped at the coaling and sand houses for replenishment. The coaling plant was served by an inclined track from which coal was discharged from hopper gondola cars. Adjacent to the roundhouse, as shown on the diagram of the CPR John Street yards, was the water tank, a conspicuous structure standing out against the sky line. The water tank stood on an openwork tower whose overall height would be 50 or 60 feet. From the base of the tower issued a flexible spout, by means of which the fireman or hostler would fill the boiler and tender tank of the locomotive run alongside. At terminals the locomotives were not watered directly from the water tower but from what were known as standing pipes supplied from the water tower, as was the case at the CPR John Street yard, the standing pipe marked SP on the diagram. At way stations, on the other hand, the locomotive was detached from the train and run under the water tower. A stores building also appears on this diagram, often annexed to the roundhouse itself but in this instance a separate building. Similarly there was a bunkhouse with sleeping quarters for off-duty engine crews. Often the bunkhouse was incorporated in the roundhouse as an annex.

The size of a roundhouse is indicated by the number of stalls (a term of equine derivation; indeed the early engine houses or sheds were known as "engine stables"). A stall consists of a segment of a roundhouse made up of one track, between the rails of which was an engine pit the width of the track and more than half the length of the stall, measured from the front entrance to the rear wall. In the Outlook, Saskatchewan, photo, spacious double windows along the rear wall at each stall can be seen through the open doors, as well as the double doors at the entrance to each stall. Above the doors may be seen the transom lights. The roof slopes from front to rear, so designed in the interests of drainage. Roundhouse doors, originally built of wood, were always hung in pairs, one pair to each stall, opening either in or out. Early CPR roundhouses were characterized by the large amount of glazing, or lights, in the doors. Many roundhouses also had windows in the side walls, but this one at Outlook had none. A principle of roundhouse design was the provision of as much natural light as possible. A close-up of an older style of stall door is shown at the CNR Toronto roundhouse at Spadina Avenue, and by contrast the newer type of metal roll-top door on the same roundhouse. The CPR West Toronto roundhouse shows, albeit less than adequately, the back wall of a roundhouse, with the turntable in the centre background (in the right foreground is a standing pipe for the taking on of water). The slope of the roof from front to rear is clearly shown. Note also the chimneys, known as smoke jacks, one for each stall, whereby smoke from the locomotive stacks was vented. Smoke jacks had bell-bottomed hoods which fitted over the locomotive stacks, a notion of which may be gained from the line drawing in profile showing a locomotive positioned under a smoke jack. Ideally, smoke jacks were constructed

17

CPR roundhouse, Outlook, Saskatchewan, June 1916.

– CP Archives

CNR roundhouse, Toronto (Spadina Avenue), showing stall doors. – photograph by author, 1982

CPR roundhouse at Havelock, Ontario.

– Brian Oates

CPR roundhouse, West Toronto, c.1915.

– CP Archives

with non-combustible and non-corrosive materials to withstand the effects of the sundry gases emitted from the locomotive chimney, but frequently were of wood, especially in the earlier period. An interior illustration of the Brandon roundhouse shows the engine pits, with the stall doors in the left background. Roundhouse floors were of cement, cinders, stone, brick, or wood blocks, and the engine pits were generally lined with cement or stone, and sometimes with brick. The engine pits were two to three feet deep, designed to give machinists, fitters and cleaners access to the underside of the locomotives. The roof was supported by wooden posts, generally of Douglas fir, the length of the stall. The older type of roundhouse had a wooden roof made up of purlins, heavy beams which ran longitudinally along the length of the stall, supported by the aforementioned vertical posts; the purlins supported the lateral rafters. On the rafters were laid boards or planks, then a waterproof layer of tar and gravel. Later roundhouses incorporated iron and finally steel trusses for roof support combinations or frameworks of members so designed as to provide maximum support; in the process the use of trusses eliminated many of the vertical posts. Another later development in the larger roundhouses, and indeed in the "square houses" as well, was the monitor roof, illustrated in the line drawing in longitudinal section of the CPR John Street roundhouse, Toronto. The monitor roof was raised above the rest of the roof, the vertical sides of the monitor being glazed to admit more light. The monitor roof was preferred to the skylight as an altogether more effective design for increasing the natural light within the engine house. A clearer concept of a monitor roof, although on one of Canada's two large-scale square houses, rather than a roundhouse, is that of the Algoma Central at Sault Ste. Marie, Ontario. A variation of the monitor, known as the saw-tooth roof, was developed in both the U.S. and the U.K., but the author has yet to encounter one in Canada. One further feature in the larger roundhouses, generally located at terminals, was the perimeter track, with small connecting turntables, running along the back wall of the roundhouse and leading into the annexed machine shop. This provided a means for trundling wheels removed from locomotives in the drop pits into the machine shop for maintenance work.[5]

To conclude this survey of the anatomy of the roundhouse, notice must be taken of the annexes forming an integral part of the roundhouse proper. Most important of these was the machine shop, located at all terminal points, where one stall might be reserved as a machine shop in lieu of an annex. Machine shops were rectangular projections of the roundhouse, with direct access thereto. More will be said in the following section about the function of the machine shop, its equipment and staff. Under the same roof, or sometimes in an adjacent but separate building, was the boiler house with its tall chimney, fitted with one or more stationary boilers for the raising of steam to operate the machinery in the machine shop before it was electrified, to provide heat for the building, and at a later date, steam for the rapid firing up of boilers. Next to the boiler rooms was found the coal storage. (By 1950 most boilers were oil fired.) A foreman's office was annexed to the roundhouse, as well as a signing in and time room for engine crews, and often a cafeteria for the staff. Invariably a locker room and lavatory were included in the sundry annexes which grew off a roundhouse like barnacles on a ship's hull. The bunkhouse for the repose of engine crews was more often than not in a separate but contiguous building. Often a storeroom for parts was included in the overall structure. Such then were the broad lineaments of the typical roundhouse on this continent.

---

5   Walter G. Berg, Buildings and Structures, op. cit., p. 173-4.

Smoke jack and roof supports in the CPR roundhouse at Brandon, Manitoba.
– Manitoba Archives

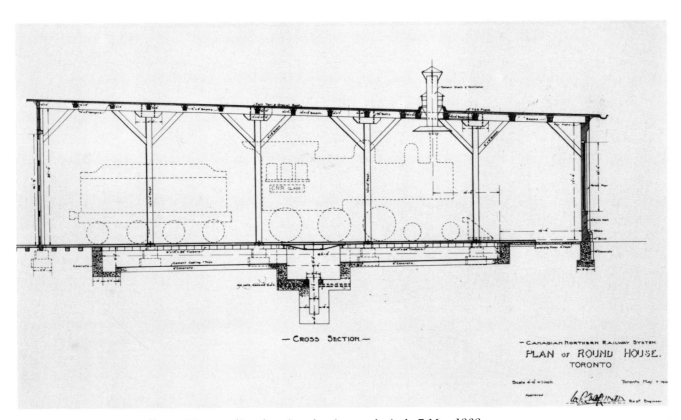

CNoR roundhouse, Toronto, line drawing showing smoke jack, 7 May 1908.
– NAC, National Map Collection

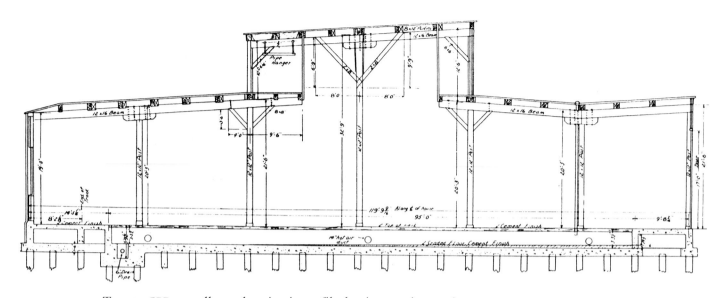

Toronto CPR roundhouse drawing in profile showing monitor roof.
– *Canadian Railway & Marine World*, Dec. 1929

Interior CPR Brandon roundhouse, 1903.   – Manitoba Archives

THE FUNCTION AND ROUTINE OF THE ENGINE HOUSE

Although what follows applied to the typical roundhouse, it is to be understood that the description fits the square house as well, in overall terms. Since by far the greater number of large engine houses in North America were roundhouses, this is the term used in the succeeding paragraphs, although it is not to be inferred that the function, organization and routine would be radically different with a large square house, such as those at Sault Ste. Marie and Hornepayne, Ontario.

Marshall Kirkman, an American authority on railway operation, writing in 1900, described engine houses simply as buildings for the shelter and repair of locomotives, where engines were cleaned, inspected and fitted for the road. At the outset a distinction must be made between the engine house and the repair shop, whose functions, at least in the case of the large engine houses, overlapped to some degree. The repair shop, located at the principal terminal of a railway, or at more than one location with a transcontinental railway, did major overhauls. The work was done to high standards, fine tolerances and there were few deadlines. The goal was little short of perfection, in order that the work need not be repeated for a considerable time. Some railroaders felt that repair shops tended to overdo the job from a practical standpoint. Quality of workmanship was the keynote in the repair shop. Repair shops, such as the famous CPR Angus shops in Montreal (opened in 1904), handled every aspect of work on a locomotive, including the design and building of locomotives from scratch. It was demanding work and it was not rushed.[6]

By contrast the role of the engine house was to service locomotives and do what was necessary in order to return the locomotive to the road in the shortest possible time. The smaller engine houses handled emergency repairs only, but the large engine houses at principal junctions and terminals took on much more than this, and indeed there was some overlap between their more elaborate repairs and that generally reserved for the repair shop. Engine house work was more hectic, working conditions were not up to the standards of the repair shop, nor was the equipment, and the urgent demands of the job put a premium on flexibility and ingenuity on the part of work crews. At some major divisional points, where there was unlikely to be a repair shop, the engine house had to assume the functions of the shops, insofar as possible. Engine house work loads fluctuated from day to day, and indeed from shift to shift, with frequent crises, short deadlines and more work than the staff could adequately handle. The work was organized in shifts around-the-clock, and until mid-century six-day work weeks were the rule.[7]

By 1911 the American Master Mechanics Association, which had carried out a survey of the principal railways on the continent, classified engine houses in three categories: those located at outlying ends of branch lines or at minor divisional points; those located at major divisional points or terminals, but without the support of a neighbouring repair shop; and finally, those engine houses at important divisional points which also had the full facilities of a repair shop. Obviously the first category would have the minimum demands made on it, and so would require less equipment, whereas the engine house at a busy junction but without the support of a repair shop would have the heaviest load and hence require more adequate facilities to meet its commitments. No consensus was arrived at regarding the plant required at the third category of engine house, that located at a busy terminal but with a fully equipped repair shop in the vicinity. As may be readily imagined, the recommended requirements for an engine house at busy divisional points but without the support of a repair shop were

---

6   Marshall M. Kirkman, *The Science of Railways,* in 12 vol., Vol. i, (New York & Chicago: World Railway Publishing Co., 1900), pp. 238-40; *Railway and Marine World,* (Toronto), July 1911, p. 587.
7   Ibid.

extensive. Such engine houses should be equipped to carry out all work short of a "backshop overhaul." The machine shop plant accordingly should have tools on hand for work on the driving rods, driving boxes, ordinary valve gear work and replacement of flues. The engine house machine shop should be equipped with a forge, a 72-inch boring mill, a driving wheel lathe, a 38-inch tire-turning lathe, a planer, slotter, bolt cutter, a 50-ton hydraulic press, a power-driven valve-setting machine, air hammers, hot water washout facilities, both 16 and 24-inch lathes, a 36-inch vertical drill, emery grinder, pipe bender, a punch and shear, and an air compressor. On the other hand, machine shops located at minor divisional points or on branch lines could generally dispense with power-driven machinery and could function with a more modest inventory: twist drills, dies, flue tools, pipe cutters, jacks, sledges, drifts, crowbars, and such basic tools as saws, brace and bits, bench shears, reamers and wrenches. Engine houses in this category would be expected to make emergency repairs only, sufficient to get a locomotive back on the road and to a major divisional shop or, if necessary, a repair shop.

The bigger roundhouses, where more complex work was done, had a larger and more specialized labour force, whereas the smaller engine houses, where only emergency repairs were handled, had a smaller and less specialized staff. The latter plants in some respects offered better experience, since the work was less specialized and in some measure a man had to be able to turn his hand to a variety of jobs, putting a premium on improvisation.[8]

C. Kyle, CPR master mechanic, read a paper in 1909 before the Canadian Railway Club, describing the organization and routine of a typical CPR roundhouse of that day. In overall charge of the roundhouse was the foreman, who organized the work and was responsible for its performance. The foreman was expected to be concerned with costs and to ensure that the work was carried out efficiently and economically, for cost accounting had become a major consideration in the operation of a railroad. The foreman's operational assistant was the chargeman or leading hand, who worked closely with the foreman on the organization of the work and who discussed with him means for increased efficiency and economy of operations. The chargeman was responsible for rendering a complete account for all mechanical failures, whether attributable to faulty materials or workmanship. Answering to the chargeman were the skilled tradesmen — machinists, boilermakers, blacksmiths, carpenters, electricians, air-brakemen — who serviced the locomotive. Under them were the apprentices in their respective trades, undergoing training and periodically writing examinations in order to qualify in turn for certification. In addition to the above tradesmen, the aristocrats of the roundhouse, were a number of semi-skilled men and simple labourers. These included engine wipers, engine cleaners, ash-pit men, light-up men, and trimmers. Finally, there was the hostler (one frequently notices the use of equine terms), who took over incoming locomotives from the crews, ran them over the ash pit, where the ash-pit men pulled the fires, onto the turntables and thence into the roundhouse. The hostler brought engines out of the roundhouse when ready for the road and parked them just beyond the turntable, where the road crew would take them over. The hostler's duties included moving the locomotives from one stall to another in the roundhouse in accordance with the maintenance schedule. The hostler acted as a go-between or link between the engine crew and the roundhouse maintenance men, and according to master mechanic Kyle, this role demanded tact on occasion.[9]

Procedure in handling locomotives naturally varied from one road to another. A 1911 issue of *Railway and Marine World* describes that procedure on the Intercolonial Railway

---

8   Ibid., pp. 587 and 589; Ernest Cordeal, *Railroad Operation* (New York: Simmons-Boardman, 1924), pp. 45, 47-9, 62 *passim.*

9   J.C. Clarke, CPR roundhouse foreman, Toronto – oral; *Railway and Marine World,* Nov. 1909, pp. 789 and 791.

Working on pit wall, Turcot roundhouse, Montreal, n.d.   – CNR Archives

(ICR). The hostler took over an incoming locomotive from the crew at the ash pit, where the fires were drawn by ash men and the hostler, who then moved the engine to the coal chute to replenish the tender, then to the sandhouse to fill the dome on top of the boiler, known as the sandbox, and finally to the water tower. From there the hostler ran the locomotive onto the turntable, operated by a turner, and so to the roundhouse. In the meantime the engineman who had brought the locomotive in filled out a report on any malfunctions of which he was aware. The machine foreman, referring to this report, assigned his men accordingly, and the roundhouse inspector checked all parts below the running board. Boilers were inspected thoroughly on the ICR after each trip, taking care to tighten the staybolts, connections and outer plates of the inner firebox. Some companies had the front end, or smokebox, opened and inspected by the boilermakers after each trip, others at regular intervals. Boilermakers also inspected the firebox inside and out. In the larger engine houses on such lines as the Chicago & North-Western, the foreman was relieved of all routine work and confined himself to investigating breakages and rendering reports to the company master mechanic and superintendent. In such establishments an assistant foreman was in charge of the mechanics or skilled tradesmen, and a sub-foreman of the hostlers or engine dispatchers, ash-pit men and wipers.[10]

By the 1920s increasing costs demanded a minimum turnaround time for each locomotive. Writing in 1924, Ernest Cordeal rated roundhouse efficiency on the prompt dispatch of locomotives ordered for duty, the cost of running repairs, the record regarding engine failures and breakdowns, and the mileage between consignment to the shops for major overhaul. With rising costs, time studies on operations were increasingly the order of the day.[11]

Work in a roundhouse was hard, dirty and dangerous, and anyone sensitive to noise level would not have stood it for long. Hours were long, with the 6-day week and 10-hour shift the norm until perhaps the late 1930s, and the hallowed institution of the coffee break unknown. Safety regulations were rudimentary. As will be plain from the work scene showing replacement of the pit wall at Montreal's Turcot roundhouse, there were no hard hats or reinforced construction boots. The industrial nurse was still in the future, although sometimes a few of the workmen were qualified in first aid. Most roundhouse veterans have grisly tales to tell of gruesome accidents. With the provision of various bridge and gib cranes this century, the work became a little less arduous, but it was always heavy and the hours long. Most of the larger roundhouses provided lunchrooms annexed to the engine house as time went on, but one suspects that frequently lunch was eaten from the lunch pail on the job, particularly when the crew was under pressure, as frequently happened in roundhouse work. Conditions were no doubt ameliorated through the work of trade unions. According to the testimony of a veteran of the CPR John Street roundhouse, Toronto, hard hats and construction boots came on the scene as safety measures only in the late 1960s.[12]

The purchasing power of the dollar has so declined over the past century that rates of pay reflect merely the relationship among the trades. GTR daily rates in 1859 indicate that pattern makers, at $1.76 per day, were the best-paid trade in the roundhouse, followed by coppersmiths and blacksmiths, and then by the fitter, or mechanic, who at $1.66 per day was fourth on the list. The boilermakers, a trade which lasted throughout the steam era, were paid $1.62 per day, and so, although performing a skilled and vital function, were seventh on the pay sheet. With changes in locomotive design and construction techniques the relationship among the trades changed, and indeed some became obsolete. For example, since copper and

---

10 Ibid., Dec. 1911, pp. 1093 and 1095; *Railroad Gazette* (New York, 19 May 1905, pp. 523-4.
11 Ernest Cordeal, op. cit., pp. 45, 47-9, 62.
12 J.C. Clarke, op. cit.

brass figured much less in the design of locomotives, brass founders and coppersmiths, skilled tradesmen in the 1850s found their services less in demand as time went on. The advance of technology called new skilled trades into existence, such as the air brakeman by the 1890s. Machinemen and strikers (assistants who wielded a heavy sledge hammer) were paid $1.01 per day, close to the bottom of the pay scale. Timekeepers and storekeepers, on the other hand, earned $1.31 per day, and woodmen $1.40, suggesting that the latter trade involved more than filling tenders (in 1859 most locomotives on Canadian roads burned wood). The stationary engineman or, as he was later known, boilerman, whose pay was $1.28 per day, lasted until the era of the oil-fired boiler. At the lower end of the scale were the pumpmen, at 98¢ per day, cleaners at 97¢, and finally labourers, who brought home just 95¢ after a 12-hour shift. Since the foregoing was long before the day of the trade union, these 1859 rates no doubt reflected merely the law of supply and demand, as well as relative skill required.[13]

---

13 Thomas E. Blackwell, *Report on the Grand Trunk Railway for 1859*, (London: Waterlow and Sons, 1860).

Great Western Railway shops, Hamilton, CW.
– Metropolitan Toronto Library Board, *Canadian Illustrated News,* 4 Feb. 1863

The Engine House in the Early Years of Canadian Railroading: 1850s-1870s

At time of writing, the first engine house on the pioneer railways of British North America cannot be identified. The Champlain & St. Lawrence Railway, opened in 1836, had but one locomotive, but whether a shelter was provided for the *Dorchester* at either end of the 14-mile line is unknown. In like manner, research into the opening of the Montreal & Lachine Railway in 1847 has elicited nothing on engine sheds. These very early railroads, with one or two locomotives, obviously would not need more than a rectangular shed or shelter at one or other of the terminals. Indeed as late as 1881 the Quebec, Montreal, Ottawa & Occidental Railway was making do with a makeshift shelter, at Hochelaga, Quebec, consisting of a cover stretched across a couple of tracks, and so it is not unreasonable to assume that engine sheds 35 to 40 years earlier were of a rudimentary design to accommodate one or two locomotives.[1]

The earliest pictorial evidence found for a roundhouse in British North America is an 1863 *Canadian Illustrated News* print of the Great Western Railway shops at Hamilton, Canada West. In the foreground is an unmistakable masonry 12-stall roundhouse with a railway track leading in from the left. Unfortunately this print is a rear view of the roundhouse. The roof design is curious in the light of subsequent development; it appears to be an early manifestation of the monitor roof. The roof construction is difficult to determine from the print, but likely was frame. No textual evidence has been found on this very early roundhouse, although a brief reference was found in an 1853 issue of the *American Railroad Journal* to an engine house, measuring 145 feet by 156 feet with accommodation for 12 locomotives, built by the GWR in Hamilton that year. From this description it has been assumed that this engine house was a rectangular engine house rather than a roundhouse. It is also described as having a machine shop annex, which the one depicted in the print had not. For these reasons the writer presumes that the two were separate structures. Reference to the first roundhouse found in the course of research was to one built by the Ontario, Simcoe & Huron Railroad in Toronto about 1853 and bounded by Brock, Front and Bathurst streets, but no further details are given in the article by the prolific railway historian Robert R. Brown. Marguerite Woodworth, in her *History of the Dominion Atlantic Railway*, published by the company in 1936, cites completion of an engine house at Richmond, Nova Scotia, on the Nova Scotia Railway in 1854, but with no description of the structure.[2]

EARLY GRAND TRUNK ENGINE HOUSES IN THE 1850S

The first solid documentation found on early engine houses is contained in Thomas E. Blackwell's *Report on the Grand Trunk Railway Company of Canada for 1859*, which describes briefly, and illustrates with draftsman's drawings, Grand Trunk engine houses then extant. Unfortunately no mention is made of the dates of construction. Since the GTR line from Montreal to Sarnia, through Brockville, Kingston, Toronto and London, was built between 1854 and 1859, these engine houses of unusual, if not unique, design in Canada were built in this period. The unusual character of these early GTR engine houses lay in their cruciform

---

1   Quebec, Legislature. *Report concerning the Quebec, Montreal, Ottawa and Occidental Railway* 1881, (Quebec: Queen's Printer, 1881), Appendix 1, p. 25 and Appendix 2, p. 50.

2   *American Railroad Journal*, (New York, J.H. Schultz), 27 Aug. 1853, p. 554; Robert R. Brown, "Ontario, Simcoe and Huron Railway," Bulletin No. 85, *Railway and Locomotive Historical Society*, 1952), March 1952, p. 38; Marguerite Woodworth, *History of the Dominion Atlantic Railway*, (Kentville, N.S.: Dominion Atlantic Railway, 1936), p. 37.

shape and inside turntables. The purpose of the interior turntables presumably was shelter from the weather, but with two notable exceptions of the installations at Sault Ste. Marie and Hornepayne, Ontario, this design was not followed in subsequent Canadian engine houses. Neither did the cruciform engine house survive in the 1860s. The interior turntable probably originated in England, for as early as 1846 the Camden roundhouse featured one. Since the GTR was built by British contractors to standards approaching British practice (these standards were typically higher and more costly than those employed by North American contractors), it can be concluded that these early engine houses are indicative of the British influence in early Canadian railway history. With the aforementioned exceptions of Sault Ste. Marie and Hornepayne, the interior turntable was not generally adopted in Canada, probably to reduce costs by using an outside turntable. Such practice would be in line with North American practice in the days of pioneer railroading, when the goal was to keep costs down.[3]

The GTR built two cruciform engine houses at Pointe St. Charles, Montreal, whose outer dimensions measured 360 by 360 feet. Each transept, or wing, was 112 feet in length, with three stub stacks in each radiating from a central 67' 6" turntable. The building was of stone.[4]

As far as is known at the present stage of research, two and possibly three engine houses were built by the Grand Trunk at its Brockville divisional point from the mid-1850s to the early 1870s, one of which apparently survived to the mid-1950s.

Undoubtedly the first engine house put up by the GTR at Brockville is clearly shown in a draftsman's plan dated 1859, which shows a cruciform engine house of frame construction with a interior 44-foot turntable. Presumably this cruciform structure was built circa 1854-55, when the GTR was constructing its line from Montreal to Toronto and Sarnia, but the date cannot be determined more precisely than that. The illustration shows a structure of maximum outer dimensions 168 by 200 feet, with tracks leading from the turntable to each of three transepts, 62 feet in width. Note that this 1859 plan shows no other engine house or shed in the Brockville yards. The date of demolition is unknown, but it may have been as early as 1870-72.

There were two GTR engine houses extant at Brockville in 1919, one of which (described as engine house number 1) by its configuration was a roundhouse, and the other (described as engine house number 2) probably a rectangular engine shed. The first measured 75 by 84 by 181 feet, with brick walls, a frame roof, and ten stalls whose doors were 16 feet in height and 14 in breadth. This roundhouse was equipped with a 60-foot air-driven turntable. The boiler room was housed in an attached annex. By this date (1919) the roundhouse was used for light locomotives only. The date of construction of engine house number 1 is not definitely established, although in part it answers the description of an engine house built in 1872 to accommodate ten locomotives served by a 60-foot turntable, but there is insufficient evidence to justify definite identification. The demolition date is unknown. The other Brockville engine house, engine house number 2, reported as extant in 1919, was described as of stone construction, 205 feet in length, with three tracks. The three stall doors measured 16 by 15 feet, and there was an annexed machine shop. This may have been the rectangular shed which fits the brief description from two other sources of an engine shed built in the 1850s and demolished circa 1955. If so, engine house number 2 was among the oldest in the country at the time of its demise about 30 years ago.[5]

3   Marcus Binney and David Pearce, op. cit., pp. 160-2 *passim*.
4   Thomas E. Blackwell, op. cit., appendices, Plan of Grand Trunk Property, Point St. Charles.
5   Thomas E. Blackwell, *Report on the Grand Trunk Railway of Canada for 1859*, (London: Waterlow & Sons, 1860), appendices, plan GTR Brockville yards; J. Norman Lowe, *Canadian National in the East*, Vol. 1, (Calgary, Alta.; British Railway Modelers of North America, 1981), p. 8; PAC. RG36, series 35, Vol. 23, Report Locomotive and Car Department, GTR, 1919; Ibid., Series 35, Boards,

Plan of GTR property, Point St. Charles, Montreal, showing cruciform engine houses. — NAC

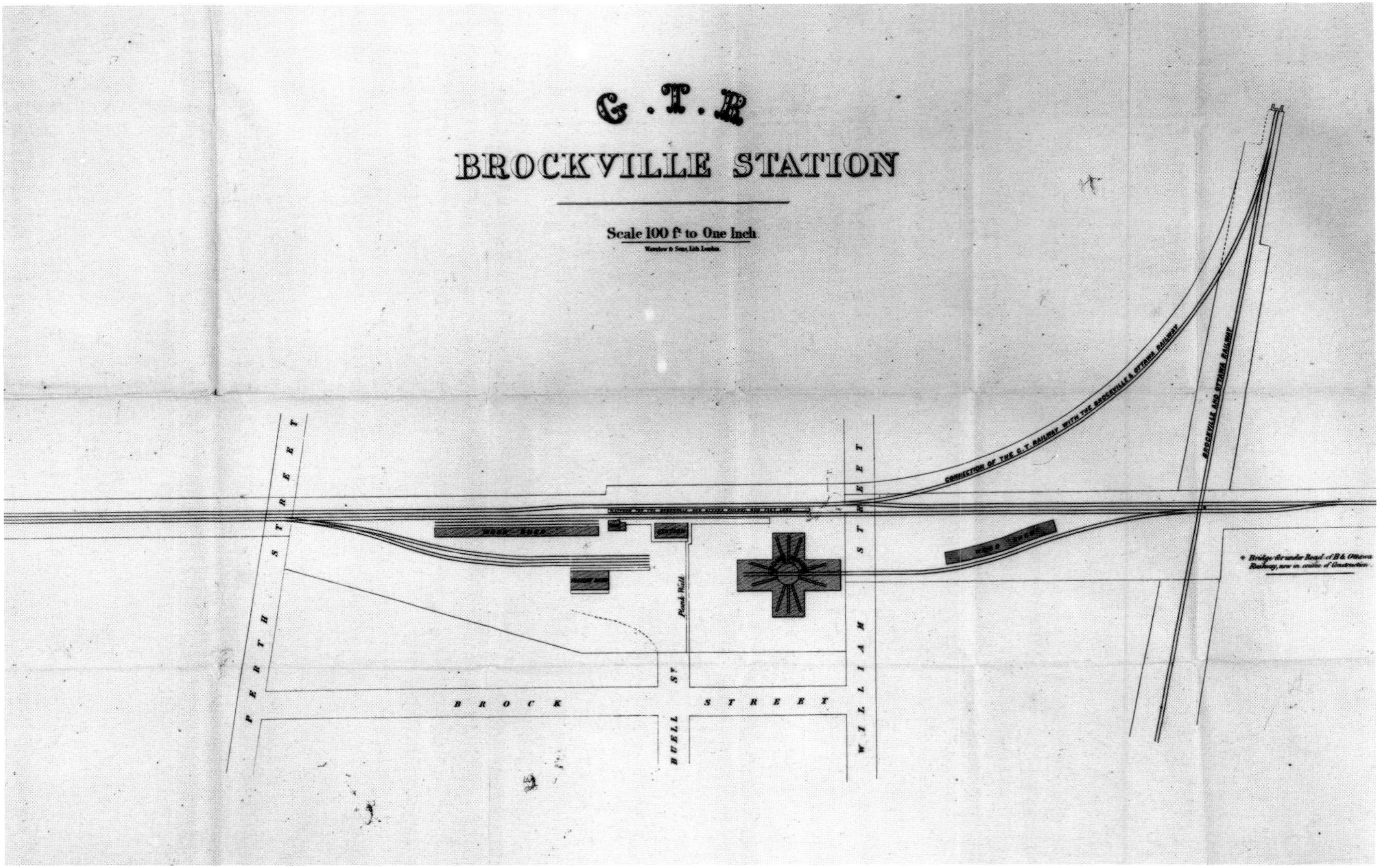

G.T.R
BROCKVILLE STATION
Scale 100 f^t to One Inch
CONNECTION OF THE G.T. RAILWAY WITH THE BROCKVILLE & OTTAWA RAILWAY
BROCKVILLE AND OTTAWA RAILWAY
PERTH STREET
WILLIAM STREET
BROCK STREET
BUELL ST
Plank Walk

Plan of GTR Brockville property showing cruciform engine house 1850s. – NAC

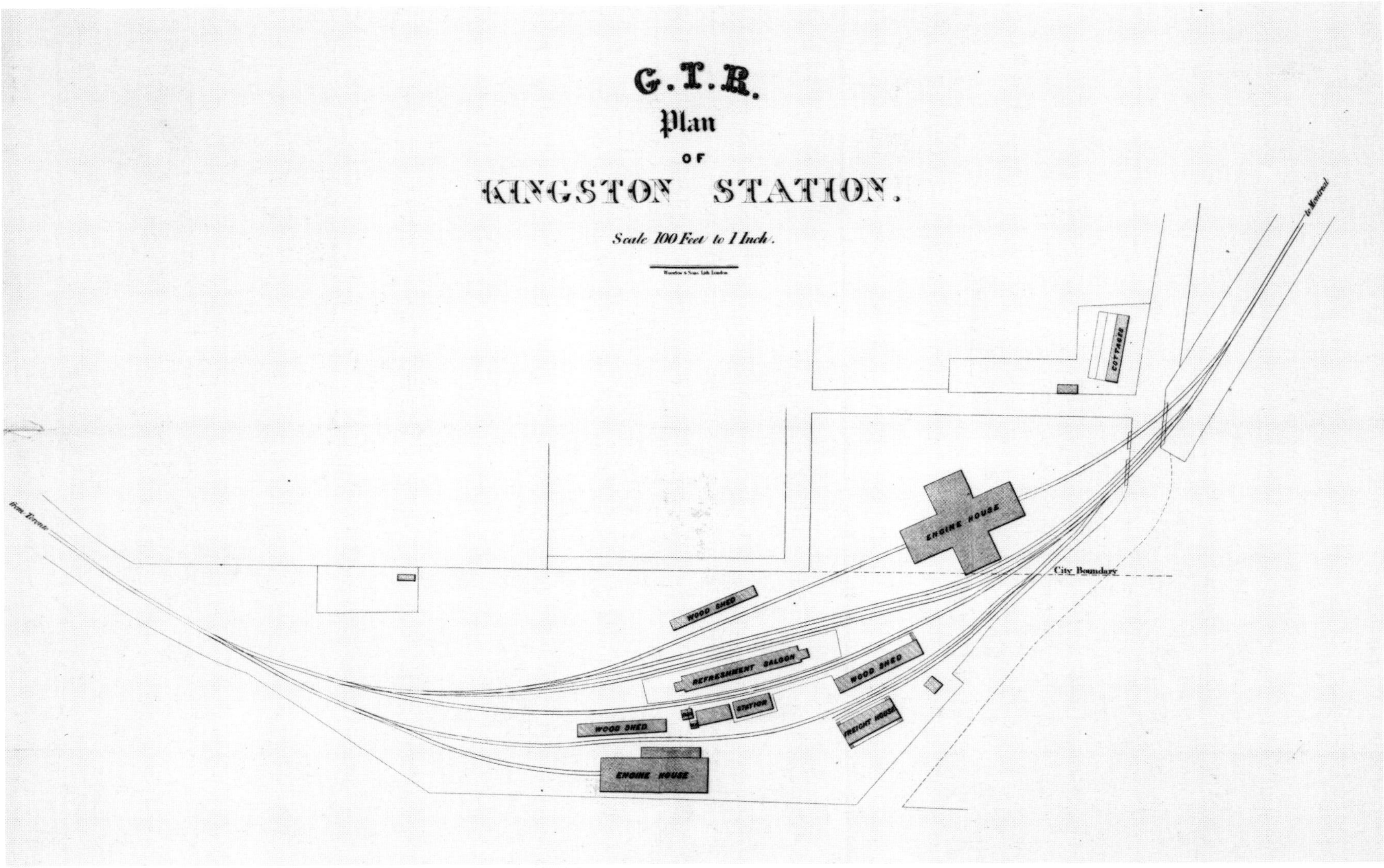
G.T.R.
Plan
OF
KINGSTON STATION.
Scale 100 Feet to 1 Inch.
to Montreal
from Toronto
COTTAGES
ENGINE HOUSE
City Boundary
WOOD SHED
REFRESHMENT SALOON
WOOD SHED
STATION
WOOD SHED
FREIGHT HOUSE
ENGINE HOUSE

Plan of GTR station and yards, Kingston, 1850s. – NAC

In Kingston, a junction point and the next divisional point west of Brockville, the GTR in the mid-1850s built another cruciform engine house, but this time of wood, measuring 200 by 162 feet at its maximum extent; the transepts, or wings if one prefers a secular term, were 62 feet in width. No turntable is shown on this plan.[6]

Cobourg in this period boasted a rectangular rather than cruciform engine house, 125 feet in length by 56 in breadth. This GTR structure was built of wood. There were three tracks within the engine house and a 44-foot turntable.[7]

The GTR Toronto terminal was equipped with a roundhouse, but no further information has been found thereon. At London, on a branch line of the GTR, a "fine brick building just outside the city limits" was built in 1858, according to the October 2 issue of the *American Railroad Journal* in anticipation of the line being opened to London the following week.[8] Another cruciform engine house, 350 by 150 feet, was built by the GTR at its Sarnia terminal.

Finally, the Blackwell *Report* includes a plan and very brief description of a rectangular engine house, with annex, apparently of wood construction, at Richmond Junction, Quebec. The engine house proper measured 150 by 100 feet, and the machine shop annex or extension, 50 by 75 feet. Neither a turntable nor a wye is shown on the plan.[9]

The Blackwell *Report* for 1859 indicates a Grand Trunk predilection for the rectangular or cruciform engine house incorporating interior turntables, at least for the smaller structures. The company also had roundhouses at both Montreal and Toronto at that time. Although it is a reasonable conclusion that the earliest railways in British North America used simple rectangular engine sheds for their limited needs, it is apparent that in Toronto and Montreal, at least by the 1850s, the roundhouse form or design had made its appearance. It rapidly became the dominant type on this continent, although not elsewhere.

Included is a plan, drawn up by the GTR in its Montreal engineers' office in September 1869, for a rectangular 3-stall engine house at Stratford, Ontario. The engine shed measured 162 feet in length by 40 feet in breadth. The design was a combination of the stub track and run-through type, with the two outer tracks ending in a buffer, or "bunter" as marked on the drawing, and the centre track a run-through. The turn table, of undisclosed length, was housed in what appears to have been a separate building. The engine shed was designed with a pitched roof supported by a simple truss; the clearance from the engine shed floor to the joist supporting the roof truss was 16 feet. There is no mention of building materials on the plan, nor is it known whether the structure was in fact built, but it is indicative of Grant Trunk concepts for small engine houses at the time.[10]

Offices, Commissions etc., Vol. 22, Field Notes RAC Henry, p. 49; *Canadian Railway & Marine World*, Dec. 1933, p. 558; Canadian Northern Railway Co., *Encyclopaedia* CNR, Engine Houses, p. 5.

6   Thomas E. Blackwell, op. cit., appendices, Plan of Kingston sta.
7   Ibid., appendices, Plan of Cobourg sta.
8   *American Railroad Journal, 2 Oct. 1858, p. 629.*
9   Thomas E. Blackwell, op. cit., appendices, Plan of Sarnia sta., *American Railroad Engineer*, 8 Oct. 1859, p. 646.
10   Thomas E. Blackwell, op. cit., appendices, Plan of Richmond Jct. sta.

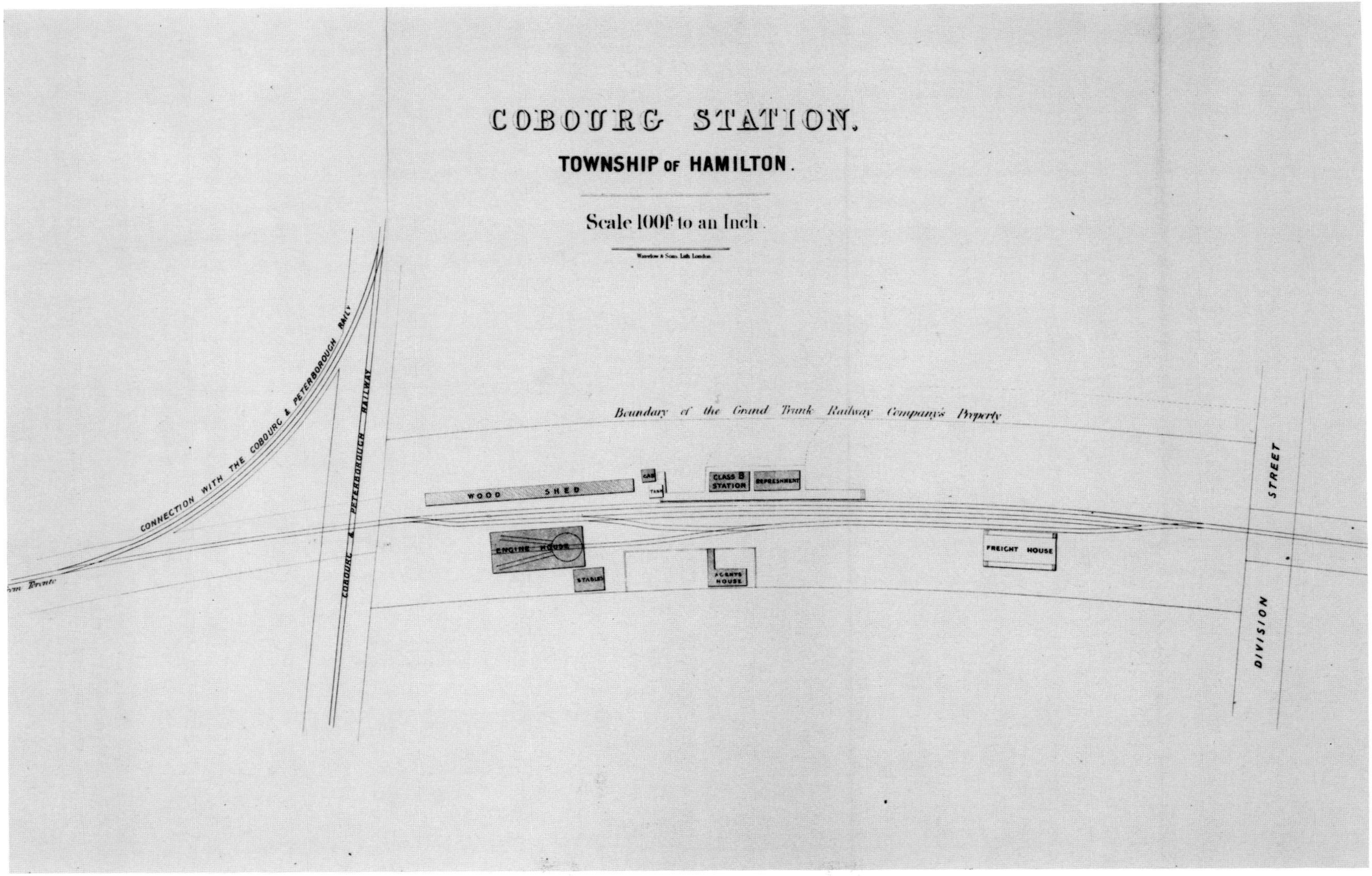

COBOURG STATION.
TOWNSHIP OF HAMILTON.

Scale 100ft to an Inch.

Waterlow & Sons, Lith London.

Boundary of the Grand Trunk Railway Company's Property

STREET

DIVISION

FREIGHT HOUSE

CLASS B STATION

REFRESHMENT

A GOODS HOUSE

CABS

WOOD SHED

ENGINE HOUSE

STABLES

COBOURG & PETERBOROUGH RAILWAY

CONNECTION WITH THE COBOURG & PETERBOROUGH RAILWAY

Plan of GTR Cobourg property showing rectangular engine house 1850s.

– NAC

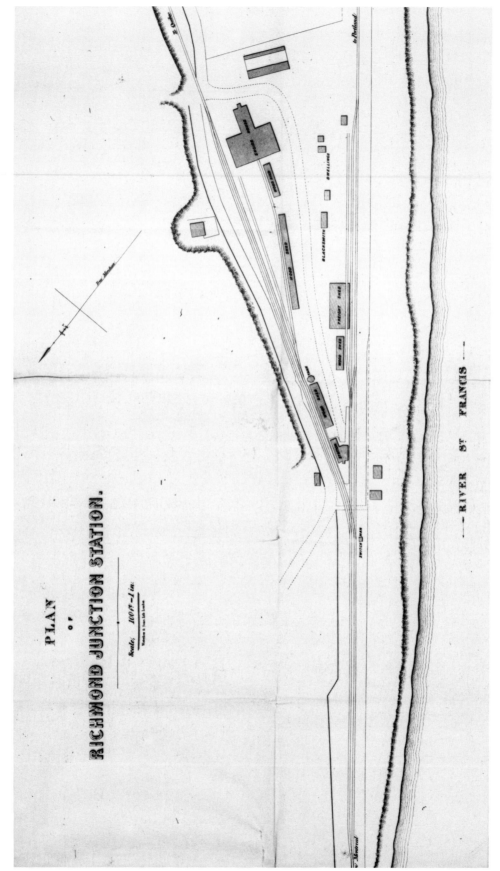

Plan of Richmond Junction GTR station and yards showing engine house, 1850s.   – NAC

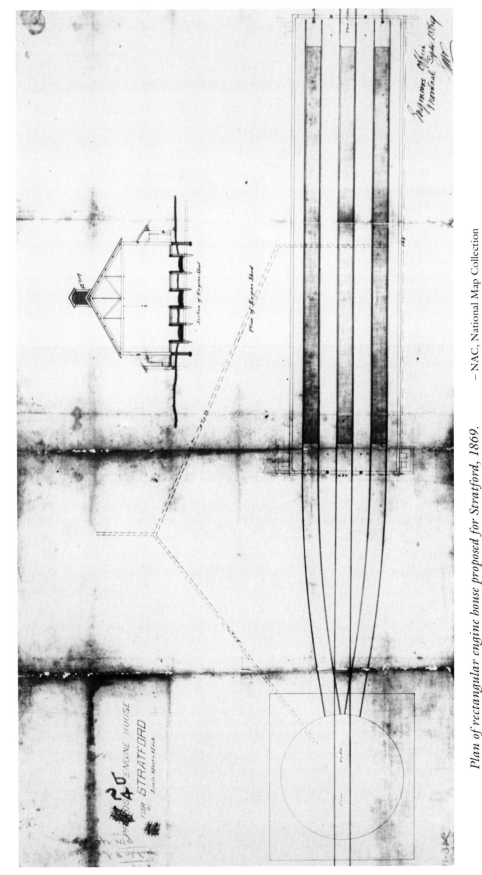

Plan of rectangular engine house proposed for Stratford, 1869. — NAC, National Map Collection

ENGINE HOUSES ON SEVERAL RAILWAYS IN THE 1860S AND 1870S

The Niagara & Detroit River Railway, made up of several small roads, was incorporated in 1858 to build a line from Niagara Falls (then known as Clifton) to Windsor. Their engine houses, designated engine stables located at terminals, were described in very general terms as "of brickwork or masonry and covered with tin or slate," with the provision of a turntable at each.[11]

The Pictou Railway (Nova Scotia) followed in some measure the GTR pattern insofar as provision of an inside turntable was concerned. In 1867 they built at Pictou a 6-stall stone engine house "of the most substantial character," with provision for an additional six stalls if needed. The reason for the interior location of the 45-foot turntable of pitch pine construction was to shelter it from the weather. Space was provided for the addition of a machine shop. Elsewhere in Nova Scotia, the Windsor & Annapolis Railway built engine sheds at both Kentville and Annapolis complete with turntables, each to house three locomotives, but no further details have been found.[12]

In 1872 William Montgomery of Halifax undertook to rebuild the walls and replace the roof of a Nova Scotia Railway roundhouse, located at Richmond, outside Halifax. This roundhouse had been built some years previously, perhaps in 1854 as noted above or 1858 when the line from Richmond to Truro was opened. The Montgomery contract gives some detail of the roof construction. The roof was made up of wooden beams trussed with iron rods, on which was laid tongue-and-groove boarding, surmounted by a 3-ply layer of felt and gravel. The roof was supported by 14 cast-iron columns, and the floor was of 2-inch spruce plank. Felt, pitch and gravel roofing was common throughout the roundhouse era, although, as will be later described, new roofing materials were introduced from time to time in the following century.[13]

The engine house at Souris, Prince Edward Island, was built by the Prince Edward Island Railway, probably in 1872. This engine house was a rectangular shed, scaled at 100 feet in length by 48 in breadth, with three stub tracks or stalls, complete with engine pits. Construction was frame throughout, except for the iron rods serving as roof trusses. There were eight windows, three on either side wall and two in the end wall. One ventilator appears in the roof. The inside turntable was 37 feet 6 inches in length.[14]

Incorporated to build a road from Quebec City to Montreal in 1853 and acquired by the Canadian Pacific Railway in 1885, the North Shore Railway planned in 1873 a total of five engine houses at Montreal, Three Rivers and Quebec City, complete with turntables. Construction was to be of stone or brick at a cost of $12,000 each, and each roundhouse was to accommodate 10 locomotives, but in 1876, when the North Shore Railway was taken over by the Quebec government, the engine houses were yet to be built. The North Shore Railway, renamed the Quebec, Montreal, Ottawa & Occidental Railway, had a stormy political career before finally being acquired by the CPR in 1885.

The foregoing information is merely an indicator of the stage of roundhouse design by the mid-1870s in Canada.[15] From these admittedly slim pickings, it appears that the round-

---

11 PAC, MG24, D16 Vol. 96, Buchanan Papers, pp. 66588-9.
12 Engineer's Office, Nova Scotia Railway, *Report on the Pictou Railway*, p. 9; Marguerite Woodworth, op. cit., p. 64.
13 PAC, RG43, C Vol. 16, Railways and Canals Records, contract 4023, p. 206.
14 PAC, RG30M, deposit 22, item 402.
15 North Shore Railway of Canada, Specifications for the Construction and Equipment of the Piles Branch, (Quebec: Augustin Coté, 185); *Contract Specifications and an Act respecting the construction of the Quebec, Montreal, Ottawa and Occidental Railway,* (Quebec: Le Canadien Steam Printing,

house, the rectangular engine house and, in the case of the Grand Trunk, also the cruciform house were common during the early years, although by the 1870s roundhouses were gaining in popularity. While frame construction was by no means uncommon, brick or stone was used in over half the roundhouses previously described, except of course for the roof. None of these structures from the pioneer period of Canadian railroading has survived.

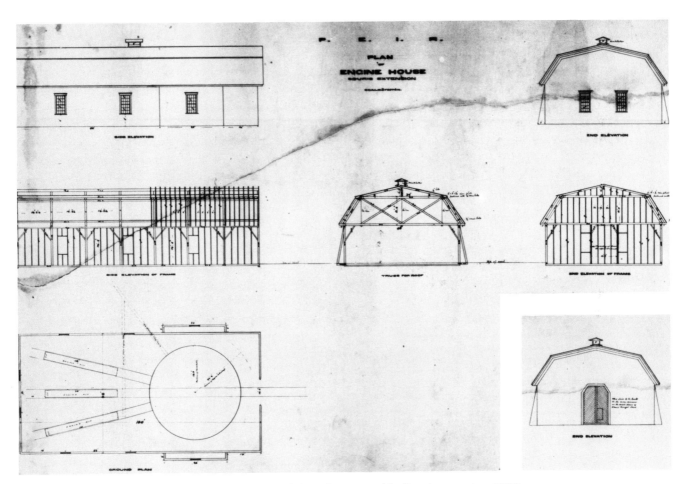

Plans of rectangular engine house with interior turntable, Souris extension, PEIR.
– NAC, National Map Collection

1876), pp. 27 and 32.

Field, British Columbia, CPR roundhouse, 1905.

The Canadian Roundhouse in the Heyday of Steam 1875-1950

The American preference for the roundhouse design rapidly spread to Canada by the 1880s. During the period covered by this chapter, spanning three quarters of a century, the roundhouse became the predominant type of engine house in Canada, expanding in size to keep pace with the steam locomotive, particularly in the era of Big Power, from about 1920 to mid-century. The roundhouse was designed to house the steam locomotive, and when the latter was superseded by the diesel at mid-century, the roundhouse itself was doomed to obsolescence. Indeed the roundhouse with its attendant turntable symbolized in its own way the power of steam, as did the locomotives it housed.

This chapter will focus on the evolution of the roundhouse, with reference first to American developments on which, in the main, Canadian designs were based. It has been observed that the Canadian pattern followed the American, to which may be added the further generalization that roundhouse design did not keep pace with that of the steam locomotive.

Roundhouse development is treated in three sections. The first covers the period 1870-1900, during which the basics of roundhouse design were established: use of stone and brick to reduce the fire hazard, introduction of roof trusses to eliminate roof columns in the interior, and improvement of fire-resistant roofing, observed at an early date on the Niagara & Detroit River Railway. The second period, 1900-19, witnessed the introduction of new construction techniques, improved fireproofing design and improved machinery, such as bridge cranes and movable cranes. The third period, 1920-50, saw the development of the completely fireproof roundhouse, increasing use of structural steel and the introduction of the trussed roof on an extended scale, steel frame construction, and the technique of direct steaming. The year 1949 marked the construction of the last roundhouse in Canada; hence the story of the roundhouse may fittingly end in 1950, after which Canadian railways were in the throes of rapid diesel conversion. By 1960 only one in ten locomotives in service on Canadian roads was steam.

Increasingly from the 1920s on, the roundhouse became a strictly utilitarian structure, devoid of architectural distinction or style. This was not so with railway stations, structures very much in the public eye and so contributing to the company's image. By contrast, roundhouses were literally low-profile, grimy structures tucked away in the yards, serving nonetheless a vital function on any railroad using steam locomotives.

The subject of roundhouse standardization also merits attention, specifically the manner in which the subject is dealt with in the following pages. Standardization is a trend common to industrial techniques, with very few exceptions. One has only to consider the steam locomotive, and in more recent times its successor, the diesel-electric, and for that matter the motor car. Roundhouse design was no exception. From 1910 and increasingly during the post-war period, roundhouses, while increasing in size and efficiency, became less distinct from one road to another. In the 1880s and 1890s CPR roundhouses were recognizable by the design of their stall doors and transoms, whereas 50 years later anyone, other than possibly an architect, would be at a loss to distinguish roundhouses on one line from those on another.

The various railway companies adopted standard designs to meet their requirements, based on the increasing size and complexity of locomotives. In the following pages use of the term "standard design" means one adopted by the company and designated as such on draftsman's plans or line drawings. A railway company might have had several standard designs for roundhouses at a particular time. For example, in 1929 the CPR had no fewer than six standard designs, according to a plan on file. On the other hand the term "standardized design" is the author's deduction, based on evidence of a number of similarly designed structures on a particular railroad. The GTR cruciform engine houses built in the 1850s, described in an earlier context, may be described as a "standardized design," based on their number, but not as a "standard design," since no such designation appears on any of the plans on file. One standard design would differ from another on the same road by the number or the length of the stalls, construction materials (the larger structures more fire resistant), and the scale of maintenance facilities available.

THE ROUNDHOUSE COMES OF AGE 1870-1900

The 1840s roundhouse at Camden, England, mentioned earlier, may not have been the first, but the date and location of the first roundhouse on this continent are unknown at time of writing. Although the square or rectangular house was preferred in Britain, the roundhouse was by no means a rarity. The Great Western Railway favoured roundhouses; both the North-Eastern Railway and the Midland built roundhouses of considerable size. At Hull there was one very unusual structure, for which the construction date is not given, but it cannot have been early; the Dairycoates engine house was made up of no fewer than six roundhouses in line and interconnected. In the United Kingdom, however, the straight shed, rectangular in shape, was the more common.[1] It is not known when the roundhouse made its first appearance in the United States. By 1870 the Chicago, Rock Island & Pacific opened one of 41-stall capacity, larger than any in Canada, with but one exception, in the whole of the steam era. The Chicago & Rock Island roundhouse at Englewood, Illinois, had 60-foot stalls, a 60-foot turntable, and measured 278 feet in diameter. An even larger roundhouse was opened by the Pennsylvania Railway at West Philadelphia in 1871, with 44 stalls and engine pits 42 feet in length. The outer brick walls, side and back, were 2 feet 6 inches thick, with pilasters inside and out. The outside lintels and sills for the windows were of cast iron. The roof was supported by a triangular system of wrought-iron trusses, and the roofing was of one-inch pine covered with slate. Heating was by means of cast-iron stoves. All in all, the West Philadelphia roundhouse was a very advanced one for its time, as witness the roof trusses, slate roofing and fire-resistant design. Only the flooring (white pine), floor joists (white oak), oak wall plates, and probably the stall doors were of wood. The chief engineer of Canada's North Shore Railway in 1875 reported that American standards for roundhouse construction called for stone foundations, stone or brick walls, and slate or metallic covering, presumably for the roof, as a safeguard against fire. Moving ahead 20 years, the Nashville, Chattanooga & St. Louis Railroad's 40-stall roundhouse, opened in 1891 at Nashville, Tennessee, featured brick construction and an iron truss roof support, with the inner circle roof (at the entrance to the stalls) supported by steel columns. An effort was made to give the Nashville roundhouse an aesthetically pleasing appearance by means of circular pilasters set in the outer wall to form a part of the circle, in the manner of a pantheon. Such aesthetic embellishments were to have short shrift in the 20th century, when increasingly stark and utilitarian structures became the norm. Two years later (1893) the East Berlin, Connecticut, roundhouse opened by the New York, New Haven & Hartford Railway featured iron roof trusses and a slate-covered roof. Likewise, heating innovation was apparent. A March 1892 issue of *Railway Master Mechanic* described the introduction of hot-blast, or hot-air, heating in the Fort Gratiot, Michigan, shops of the Chicago & Grand Trunk Railway, an innovation which would largely replace stoves and direct-steam heating in roundhouses across the continent. This may be counted as one of the more significant developments of the 1890s.[2]

---

1   Marcus Binney and David Pearce, op. cit., pp. 160-2, 164-5, 167, 171 *passim.*
2   *Railroad Gazette* (New York), 17 Dec. 1870, p. 265; North Shore Railway, *Report of the Chief Engineer upon the situation, 4th March 1875,* Appendix No. 1, p. 13; *Railroad Gazette,* 18 Feb. 1871, p. 493; *Railway Review,* 14 March 1891, p. 165; *Railroad Gazette,* 3 March 1893, p. 167; *Railway Master*

CPR Roundhouses In The 1880s

Accompanying illustrations show the distinctive style of the early CPR roundhouse in the striking and handsome design of the stall doors. These were glazed for over half their height, above which was generally a triangular configuration of transom lights. An alternative design appears in the photographs of the Field, British Columbia, roundhouse in which the stall doors were surmounted by a rounded arch, without transom lights. The Field roundhouse, precise date of construction unknown, is extant. The Owen Sound, Ontario, roundhouse displays the same distinctive door design as CPR roundhouses built before the turn of the century. With no documentation the construction date of the CPR Owen Sound roundhouse is pure surmise, but could not have pre-dated 1883, when the CPR acquired the Toronto, Grey & Bruce Railway terminating at Owen Sound.

Winnipeg, Manitoba. Opened in the spring of 1883, the Winnipeg CPR roundhouse, depicted in the print after JMW Jones Co., was one of the very early roundhouses built on the transcontinental. Unfortunately this handsome print shows only the back wall of the roundhouse, hence the front entrance cannot be compared with those of other CPR round-houses of the same period. The Winnipeg roundhouse was begun in June 1882 and built in a little under a year. Its 36 stalls formed nearly a complete circle, with a diameter of 300 feet, centred on a 56-foot turntable. The roundhouse was set on a stone or masonry foundation, and the walls were of brick. The front was described as constructed of wood and glass, indicative that the wooden doors had the extensive glazing, or lights, characteristic of the company's roundhouses in its early years. Annexed to the west side of the roundhouse was an L-shaped machine shop. The roofing of both roundhouse and machine shop was described as fireproof, and this was a highly significant feature at this early date. The whole structure had steam heat. The boiler room, probably attached directly to the machine shop, had four boilers, only two of which were used in summer. Annexed to the machine shop, and forming one complex, was a blacksmith's shop, a tin and coppersmith's shop, a moulding shop, lamp room and engine room.[3]

The machine shop was equipped with a double-headed lathe for turning steel tires of driving wheels, a car axle lathe and a number of smaller lathes. The boiler room had a punching and shearing machine, and steel rollers for rolling out boiler plate. The blacksmith's shop was equipped with 14 forges and a large steam hammer.[4]

Winnipeg was at that time the major terminal in the construction of the CPR, and this roundhouse was apparently equipped for what railroaders called "backshop" work, later reserved for locomotive repair shops. The two design features which distinguished it as an up-to-date structure were the fireproof roof and the steam heat.

Other CPR Roundhouses of the 1880s. The North Bay roundhouse (dating from about 1884) was of 15-stall size, with the lights or glazing extending halfway down the doors, as characteristic of the time. The 12-stall Donald, British Columbia, roundhouse, photo-graphed about 1889, exhibits the same style, presenting an impressive aspect. The side wall appears to be of frame siding, but there is insufficient detail to confirm that feature. The Field, British Columbia, roundhouse, attributed to the late 1880s or early 1890s, of stone or masonry construction, exhibits a variation in frontal design. This 1905 photograph shows a rounded arch over the stall entrance, but the doors, although rounded at the top to conform,

---

Mechanic, March 1892, p. 42.

3   *Winnipeg Daily Sun*, 15 Sept. 1883. In passing, the attractive pen and ink sketch of an early Winnipeg CPR roundhouse cannot be identified with the one built in 1883, for apparently the CPR had more than one roundhouse in Winnipeg. In any case the sketch shows the stall doors, with the transom lights in the distinctive early CPR style.

4   Ibid.

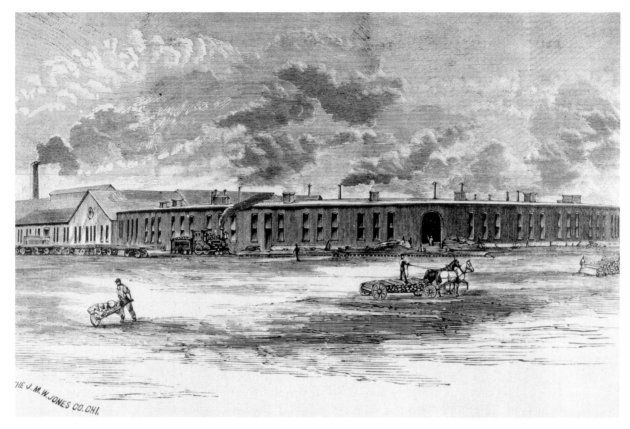

Old print of CPR Winnipeg roundhouse, c.1883. — Manitoba Archives

Print of one of the CPR roundhouses at Winnipeg, c.1890. — Manitoba Archives

Donald, British Columbia, CPR roundhouse, c.1889.   – CP Archives

Newly completed CPR roundhouse at North Bay, Ontario.   – NAC

CPR roundhouse, Owen Sound, Ontario, n.d. — CP Archives

Stone six-stall roundhouse on the CPR at Lake Louise, Alberta, June 7, 1916. — CP Archives

CPR engine house at Smiths Falls, Ontario.   – CP Archives

CPR Pacific #1278 being towed from the Smiths Falls, Ontario, roundhouse. This engine still survives in the United States.
                                                                                              – Donald E. Starr

Roundhouse, Goderich, Ontario. — CPR Archives

CPR engine house and bunk house at Megantic, Quebec, 1914. — CPR Archives

display the CPR style of glazing, extending two thirds of the distance from the top of the door. Unfortunately no documentary description has been found for the Field roundhouse.[5]

The researcher is better served in the case of the CPR roundhouse at North Bend, British Columbia, in the scenic Fraser Canyon. The North Bend structure was a 10-stall engine house built by Willson and McCrady in 1885. The foundation was of rubble masonry and the walls of brick. The contract specifications prescribed a plinth course of dressed stone, 18 inches deep and 9 wide, on the outer face of the wall (a plinth is a projecting square base of a wall or column). A stone sill was built for each window, of dimensions 7 by 3 feet, two for each stall on the back, or outer, wall. The floor beams, flooring, door posts, roof joists, and doors were all of Douglas fir. The smoke jacks and cowls, or hoods, were of iron plate. The engine pits were lined with what is described as "random" rubble masonry, laid in "hydraulic cement mortar." The turntable pit was lined with masonry of "a heavier class of stone," and the turntable, unpowered, was operated manually (probably by one man). Finally, all woodwork was to have two coats of anti-corrosive paint and linseed oil. Such was the original North Bend roundhouse, presumably of similar design to those illustrated from the preceding paragraph.[6]

Carleton Place, Ontario, Roundhouse. Notwithstanding suggestions that the extant Carleton Place roundhouse was built as early as 1859, the stall doors in the photo unmistakably in the CPR style suggest that this structure dates from the 1880s. An all but illegible stone inscription over the machine shop entrance appears to read "AD 1887, built by J.W. Munro, contractor Pembroke." In any event, the roundhouse is one of the oldest extant roundhouses in the country.

The reader is referred to an undated line drawing of the Carleton Place roundhouse in both plan and profile, and to accompanying profile drawings. It will be observed that the machine shop, a rectangular structure approximately 215 feet in length by 58 in width, extends tangent fashion across the back of the roundhouse proper. The Carleton Place roundhouse numbers 15 stalls, each 75 feet in length, with 45-foot engine pits; the stalls are 14 feet wide at the entrance and a little over 18 feet along the back wall. The roof slopes gently from front to rear at a gradient of 1:7. The 50-foot turntable has long been removed and the pit filled in. The present proprietors, the Canadian Wool Growers Association, who acquired the building in 1942, have erected a shed-like structure for the processing of wool on the site of the former turntable. The machine shop roof is peaked and supported by trusses. The foundations go down about 5 feet. The stall doors were 16 feet in height. These have all been filled in by the present owners. Heavy timbers serve as vertical posts for the roof of the roundhouse at 24-25 foot intervals.[7]

The Carleton Place roundhouse and annexed machine shop served in fact a function much beyond that of a conventional structure at an important divisional point and junction. The machine shop annex was a repair shop where major overhauls were undertaken akin to

---

5   Omer S.A. Lavallée, *Van Horne's Road*, (Montreal: Railfare, 1974), p. 107; Canadian Pacific Corporate Archives, print No. A1752 or 17835; Ibid., photo No. 2749. Apparently at one time there were two roundhouses at Field, the location of one of which was one mile west of Field (see Appendix B). *Van Horne's Road* offers a partial explanation (see pages 176-7, 1881) for this apparent anomaly. As originally constructed in 1884, the CPR line was routed through Muskeg Summit, about 2 miles west of Field, where a roundhouse may have been built. In 1902 the line was rerouted, via what was known as the Ottertail Diversion, along the river level west of Field, hence reducing the grade. The original line through Muskeg Summit was then abandoned. Lavallée is not sure whether a roundhouse was built or not at Muskeg Summit, but the possibility that one was may offer an explanation for the second roundhouse in the immediate vicinity.

6   PAC, RG43 C, Vol. 28, Railways and Canals records, contract No. 7824, p. 5701.

7   CPR Archives, Montreal, engineer plan room, line drawing.

Carleton Place roundhouse, n.d.

CPR machine shop men, Carleton Place, lunch break, 1901.

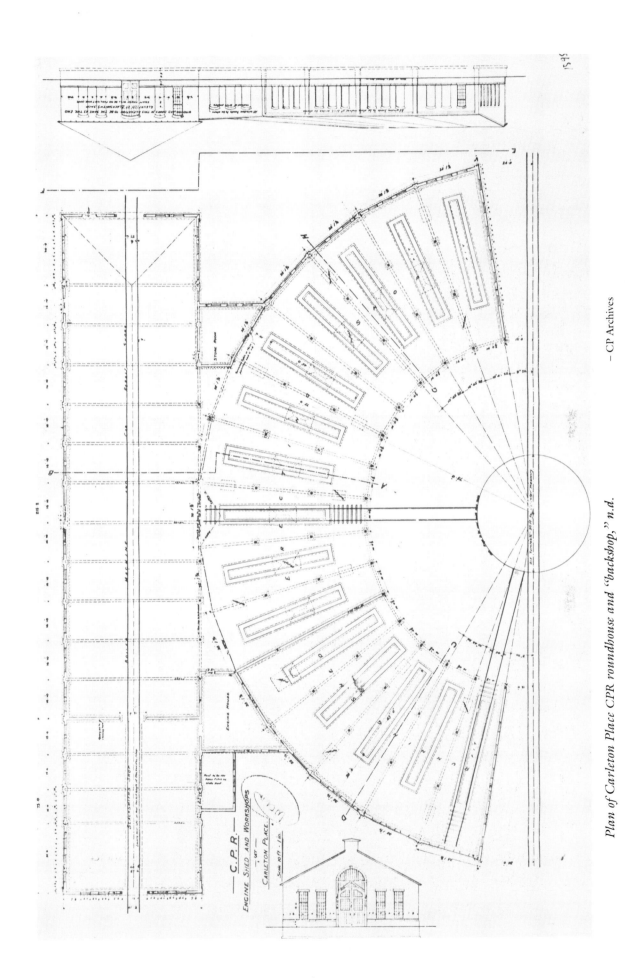

Plan of Carleton Place CPR roundhouse and "backshop," n.d.

– CP Archives

51

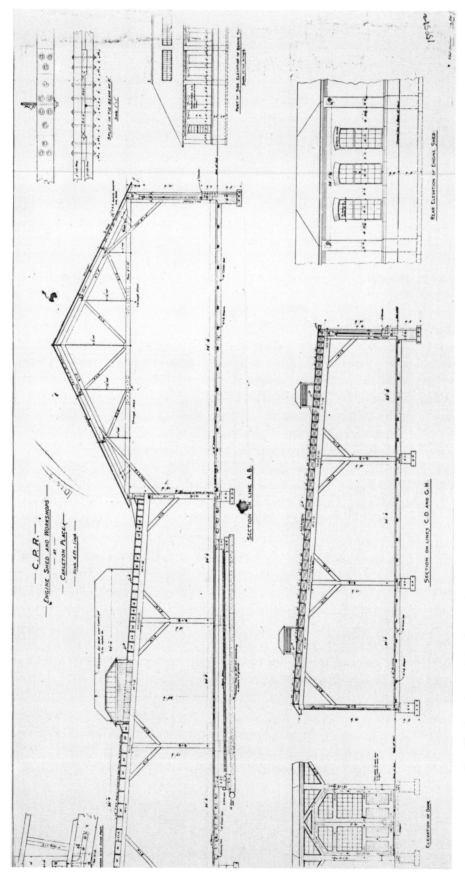

Profile drawings of Carleton Place roundhouse and shops, n.d.

– CP Archives

those at a terminal, and half the roundhouse portion served as an erecting shop for locomotives which had been literally torn down and reassembled. Only five stalls were designated as a "running shed," which was the normal function of a roundhouse, where locomotives were taken in for routine maintenance and repairs, then returned to service as soon as possible. The rest of the roundhouse, ten stalls, comprised the "erecting shop," where locomotives scheduled for overhauls were taken apart, in the sense at least of having their wheels removed, the parts trundled into the machine shop where the work was done, then the parts returned to the erecting shop for reassembly. The machine shop section was known at the time as the "backshop," where practically everything short of initial design and construction was carried out.

The backshop consisted of the rectangular space, with entrances at either end, behind the semi-circular roundhouse proper. Housed in the backshop were the boiler room, air brake room, carpenter's shop and tin shop. Along the back wall were arranged all manner of belt-driven power tools, such as lathes and punches, and finally in one corner of the backshop, the blacksmith's shop with forge. The engine room housed an air compressor, the only remaining evidence of which is a groove in the floor to accommodate the 6-foot flywheel. All this machinery was originally driven by steam and subsequently electrified at an undetermined date in the early years of the century. Originally the shops and roundhouse employed 125 to 130 men, a group of whom are seen at lunch break in a 1901 photograph, but by the time the CPR closed the facility in August 1939, the work force had shrunk to only 27 men. The Canadian Wool Growers Association acquired the property in 1942 and have used it as a warehouse ever since, with the turntable removed. This conversion probably accounts for the historic structure's survival.[8]

Sundry Roundhouses Late 19th Century
A roundhouse was built for the Northern Pacific & Manitoba Railway in 1889 by contractors Rourla and Cuns in Winnipeg. It was brick on a 3-foot concrete foundation and, at a cost of $15,700.40, measured 241 feet by 100 feet overall. This 10-stall house had a concrete floor and an annexed blacksmith's and car repair shop, the former of dimensions 71 by 56 feet. In the 1920s this roundhouse was known as the Winnipeg Joint Terminal Roundhouse and was described as a "standard second-class Northern Pacific roundhouse." When demolished sometime in 1924-25 it was known as the oldest extant structure of its type in western Canada.[9]

In the summer of 1889 Rhodes, Curry and Company undertook construction of a roundhouse and locomotive erecting shop at Moncton, New Brunswick, for the aggregate sum of $75,344. The 28-stall engine house contract called for brick walls, stone engine pits, and steam heat conveyed through 4-inch wrought-iron pipe. This structure does not impress one as being of particularly advanced design, but the specifications for brick walls and stone engine pits reflect recommended practice in the use of noncombustibles.[10]

In September 1899 the GTR opened the largest roundhouse on its system, at the east end of the Sarnia Tunnel, connecting Sarnia with Port Huron, Michigan. Numbering 30 stalls, the Sarnia roundhouse was constructed of brick on a stone foundation with a gravelled roof.[11]

In summing up roundhouse progress in Canada in the last quarter of the 19th century, it would appear that stone and brick gained general acceptance as building materials. The CPR, and perhaps the GTR and ICR, had made a start on fire-resistant roofing. There was as yet,

8   Mr. Willard, retired CPR blacksmith, Carleton Place. Ont.
9   Rodger Guinn, Research Bulletin No. 126, Parks Canada.
10 PAC, RG43 C, Vol. 30, contract No. 9920.
11 *Railway and Shipping World*, Sept. 1899, p. 266; Ibid., June 1898, p. 100.

A modern concrete addition has been made to the original 5-stall brick roundhouse on the CPR at Trois-Rivieres, Quebec, 1918.

– CP Archives

however, little use of the metal truss for roof support, apart from the Carleton Place shops. Heavy timbers continued in use as vertical roof posts, roof rafters and purlins throughout the 19th century in the United States as in Canada, and tar and gravel roofing was in widespread use in both countries. Slate roofing had been introduced in the U.S., but evidence of it in the construction of Canadian engine houses has not been found, nor does hot-blast heating seem to have been adopted in Canada before the turn of the century.

THE ROUNDHOUSE OF THE EARLY 20TH CENTURY: 1900-20

As the 1890s merged into the 20th century, the roundhouse on this continent underwent continuous development in an effort to keep pace with the steam locomotive. In general terms roundhouses expanded in size and employed new materials of a noncombustible nature in their design. Reinforced concrete, fireproof ceilings and new equipment which made shop work both less arduous and less hazardous were introduced. Electric light became the rule rather than the exception, and the monitor roof considerably improved the natural light in the larger roundhouses. Although much had been done in the 1880s and 1890s, it was nonetheless contended by some Americans that roundhouse development lagged behind that of the locomotive.

State Of The Art At The Turn of The Century And After

In 1901 the American Railway Master Mechanics Association described the laggard pace of roundhouse development in the U.S. Three general comments stand out: insufficient size, defective lighting and ventilation, and primitive facilities. The association's recommendations covered a wide range of design and construction features: steel roof trusses to eliminate intermediate columns in the interior, concrete and metal ceilings, vitrified brick paving, steel rolling doors to replace swinging wooden ones, electric light, monitor roof design, and heating either by steam pipes or hot-air blast, with the latter preferred. The hot-blast system could serve both as heating and ventilation. Oil lights and gas jets were definitely inferior to electric lighting. Smoke jacks were too often ineffective. The recommended length for engine pits was 50 to 60 feet, with a width of 4 feet and depth of 2 to 3 feet. Concrete or brick floors in the engine pits were favoured. There should be provision of overhead trolleys, portable cranes, pneumatic or electric jacks, and hoists for handling of heavy parts. Roundhouse stalls should be a minimum length of 80 feet, for many locomotives were 65-70 feet in length. Since 80-foot stalls could not be sufficiently illuminated by windows on the outer wall and stall doors, however spacious, the monitor roof was recommended to increase the natural light. The Master Mechanics Association did not favour skylights, which had a tendency to leak. The consensus among the Master Mechanics favoured a vitrified brick floor laid in a bed of sand. Roundhouse doors should be of minimum dimensions 16 by 12 feet and should be glazed on the upper portion to the limit imposed by structural design, as practised by the CPR for a number of years. These were the general features the American Master Mechanics looked for in a roundhouse in the early years of the 20th century. It may be assumed that only a few structures in the U.S. at the time came up to this standard, and that many of the smaller roundhouses at minor divisional points and on branch lines fell well short of it.[12]

Early in 1903 the New York Central Railway opened a 30-stall roundhouse at Rensselaer, New York, chiefly remarkable for having been completed in 60 days. The walls were of brick on a concrete foundation, in itself unremarkable by this date, but of significance was the provision of firewalls at 10-stall intervals. Heating was by hot air and 10-candle-power electric

---

12 *Engineering News,* (New York: Engineering News Publishing Co.), 22 Aug. 1901, pp. 120-1 *passim,* 122; PAC, MG30, B86, Barnett Coll., new Vol. 81, category 3.

lights were fitted throughout, with each engine pit equipped with a plug for a portable light. That same year the Norfolk & Western Railway opened a roundhouse at Portsmouth, Ohio, featuring the hot-blast system of heat, in which the hot air was piped to each engine pit; in the summer the fan operated without any steam in the heater, thus providing ventilation. B.F. Sturtevant of Boston supplied the heating equipment for both this roundhouse and the one at Rensselaer. This equipment acted as a fog preventive in cold weather. An improved smoke jack put in an appearance at the McKees Rocks roundhouse on the Pittsburgh & Lake Erie Railway in 1903. This smoke jack discharged smoke from the locomotive stack more efficiently.[13]

Until the advent of the direct-steaming technique in the late 1920s, the smoke jack was essential at each stall, otherwise the roundhouse would be quickly filled with suffocating, if not asphyxiating, smoke. Understandably, efforts were not spared to improve these stacks protruding 3 to 4 feet above the semicircular roofline of every roundhouse, with their bell-shaped hoods projecting down from the roof over each and every engine pit. In 1880 the average smoke jack consisted of a sheet-iron pipe or flue, 20 to 24 inches in diameter, with a bell-shaped retractable hood at its lower end inside the roundhouse. As locomotives increased in size greater strain was put on the smoke jacks, necessitating the use of more durable materials such as galvanized sheet iron, terra cotta pipe, and cast iron.

As more repairs were undertaken in roundhouses, locomotives were shifted back and forth, calling for elongated engine hoods. These hoods were first fashioned of wood, then of asbestos lumber. Hooded cast-iron jacks appeared about 1906, but in 1924, a few years before the advent of direct steaming, wooden smoke jacks were still in use, composed of laminated redwood and fir, fire-resistant but not fireproof; by this time asbestos and transite smoke jacks were available, which were fireproof and no heavier than wood. Concrete jacks in pre-cast units were also available by the 1920s.[14]

Late in 1907 a roundhouse especially designed for severe winter weather was opened by the Northern Pacific Railway at Dilworth, Minnesota. The design was developed by Northern Pacific's former mechanical superintendent, David VanAlstyne, in order to handle engines more expeditiously in cold weather. Provision was made for the drawing of the fires at any engine pit in the house. Locomotives were brought directly into the roundhouse off the road, stopping only for coal, water and sand. This was affected by combining the engine and ash pits by means of two sub-pits. Each sub-pit was filled with water and fitted with metal pans for the reception of the ashes, which were removed by means of an electric travelling hoist, conveying the contents to a cinder car running on a track around the front of the roundhouse, which in turn removed the ashes from the roundhouse. The electric hoist operated on an overhead I-beam attached to the roof trusses. An underground blow-off system was installed between the pits for discharge into the sewers. Filling and wash-out pipes for the boilers extended throughout the house, suspended from the bottom members of the roof trusses, with drops for use at each engine pit. Research on this project did not indicate that the sub-pits were ever adopted in Canada, where the outside ash pit on the approach track was a regular feature. As would be expected with the climate prevalent over so much of Canada, engine-house designers made provision for cold weather operation, but the sub-pit apparently was not taken up.[15]

---

13 *Railroad Gazette*, 20 Feb. 1903, pp. 128-9; Ontario Archives. Andrew Merilees Coll., MU 3429; *Railway and Locomotive Engineering*, (New York: Angus Sinclair Co.), July 1903, p. 335; *Railroad Gazette*, 28 Aug. 1903, pp. 614-5; *Railway and Locomotive Engineering*, Nov. 1903, p. 493.
14 *Railway Engineering and Maintenance*, Nov. 1924, pp. 450-1.
15 *American Engineer and Railroad Journal*, (New York), Nov. 1907, pp. 424-6 *passim*.

In 1910 the Pennsylvania Railroad opened the largest roundhouse (52 stalls) built up to that time, at East Altoona, Pennsylvania. Only one larger, CNR's Turcot roundhouse at Montreal, was built in Canada, although with only 40 stalls when opened in 1906. The East Altoona roundhouse was equipped for all manner of repairs short of a complete overhaul. A feature was four electrically-driven drop tables for the removal of driving wheels.[16] The use of reinforced concrete, introduced early in the 20th century, was perhaps the most significant advance in engine-house construction during this period. This technique, long since a commonplace, involves reinforcing concrete with a core of steel rods, steel mesh, or whatever serves best for giving concrete the strength it would otherwise lack. Joseph Monier, a French gardener, is credited with being one of the pioneers in the technique as long ago as 1868. The technique was introduced in roundhouse construction about 1908. *Engineering News* was to be found extolling its qualities in its April 1st issue. Reinforced concrete, which also went by the names ferroconcrete and steel concrete, was more suitable for large structures than small. Strength (a much thinner wall having equivalent strength to one of straight concrete), durability and its non-combustible nature were some of the advantages offered. However, plain concrete and brick were cheaper. Reinforced concrete by no means supplanted other building materials, such as plain concrete, brick or plaster, depending on requirements, but nonetheless the fact remains that reinforced concrete was increasingly used for construction of all types from the early years of the present century. One has only to consider skyscrapers and lighthouses, to name but two structures, whose height and resultant stresses no doubt called for reinforced-concrete design to a much greater degree than the squat and low-lying roundhouse. The same issue of *Engineering News* found brick to be more satisfactory and a little cheaper than plain concrete. Indeed a reinforced plaster wall, stiffened with steel rods, was the most economical construction and could be put up faster than concrete. The Elgin, Joliet & Eastern Railway's roundhouse, located at Joliet, Illinois, utilized reinforced-concrete beams in its roof structure, supporting monolithic concrete slabs $3\frac{1}{2}$ to $4\frac{1}{2}$ inches thick as roofing. Possibly the first roundhouse built entirely of reinforced concrete was that of the Atchison, Topeka & Santa Fe Railway at Riverbank, California, in 1912. The builders used a technique said to be unique at the time, in which the concrete was pre-cast around the reinforcing steel in a number of individual moulds. When the concrete had set, the pre-cast units were lifted from the moulds by a crane and assembled at the site.[17]

Railways had been rightly concerned about fire in roundhouses well before the turn of the century. The New York Central's East Buffalo 26-stall roundhouse (1908) was designed with two interior firewalls and steel fire doors, and the smoke jacks, made of a compound of asbestos and magnesia, were fireproof. On the other hand the East Buffalo roundhouse had interior roof supporting columns of yellow pine, roof trusses of timber and wooden doors, all of which were combustible. In this respect, as seen in the succeeding section, the New York Central may have been anticipated by both the Canadian Northern, which claimed a fireproof roundhouse as early as 1901, and the CPR.[18]

---

16 *Railway Age Gazette,* Aug. 1910, p. 244.
17 *Encyclopaedia Britannica,* 11th ed., Vol. 6, pp. 837-8; *Engineering News,* 2 April 1908, pp. 366-7; *Railway Age Gazette,* (New York), Sept. 1911, pp. 597-8; *Railway Engineering and Maintenance of Way,* RCC(Chicago), Jan. 1913, p. 13.
18 *American Engineer and Railroad Journal,* Jan. 1909, pp. 3, 5 and 9 *passim.*

Canadian Roundhouses To 1920

In this section, roundhouse construction techniques are studied on five railways, principally during the expansive period covering the first two decades of this century.

The CPR. As early as 1900 the CPR announced that the stalls in both its Field and Revelstoke roundhouses were to be rendered fireproof, and in 1904 that all future roundhouses would be completely fireproof. Details of the construction techniques used were shown in a 1902 issue of *Railway and Marine World*.[19]

A CPR standard roundhouse design, dating from 1904, featured brick, masonry or concrete construction, roofs of concrete and steel supported by steel posts, and the important provision of brick firewalls.

The North Bay roundhouse, built in 1903, replacing an earlier one, was set on a stone foundation 10 feet deep. The walls were of Arnprior limestone, with window sills of a dark sandstone. The contract was let to Munro and Company, who sublet the roof contract to J.B. Brennan of Montreal. The brief description in the September 1903 issue of *Railway and Shipping World* gives no further details, other than that initially the roundhouse would form only half a circle, but would be expanded as required.[20]

More detail is given on the CPR's new roundhouse at Winnipeg, opened in the summer of 1904. This 42-stall structure was subdivided into four sections by firewalls. The walls were of stone, brick and concrete construction, the columns supporting the roof were of reinforced concrete, as were the roof (3-inch slabs) and supporting crossbeams or purlins. To prevent condensation, an air space was left between the inner and outer slabs forming the roof. The roof columns at the stall entrances, or on the inner circle (13-feet-7-inch centres), as well as those at the back of the stalls on the back wall or outer circle (25-foot centres), were of steel. It would seem from this description that the Winnipeg roundhouse was indeed fireproof, anticipating in this respect the Riverbank, California, roundhouse on the Atchison, Topeka & Santa Fe, opened in 1912, not to mention the Joliet, Illinois, structure described in *Railway Age Gazette* in 1911. The floor of the new Winnipeg roundhouse was of brick laid in sand. Electric lighting, with three 16-candle-power drop lights for each engine pit, was incorporated, as were socket outlets in each roof column to plug in hand lights. The roundhouse was heated by hot-blast, recognized for at least ten years as superior to direct-steam heat. According to the same sources, the CPR had seven roundhouses of similar design under construction at this time: North Bay, Ontario, with 18 stalls; Ignace, Ontario (12); Brandon, Manitoba (18); Medicine Hat, Alberta (18); Swift Current, Saskatchewan (10); Moose Jaw, Saskatchewan (10); and North Bend, British Columbia (6).[21]

The CPR's Ottawa West roundhouse, 21-stall capacity, was built in 1911 by J.B. Sanderson, an Ottawa contractor. In 1925 the machine shop was modernized and in the following year a 6-stall extension was added. The walls were of reinforced-concrete construction, as were the columns and beams. The joists on the other hand were of white pine and B.C. fir. In July 1933, in the depths of the Depression, agreement was reached with the CNR for joint use of the CPR's Ottawa West roundhouse to house road engines, and of the 27-stall all-wood CNR roundhouse for yard engines of both companies; the CPR roundhouse was deemed much the more up-to-date because of the aforementioned features, although perhaps less conveniently located.[22]

---

19   *Railway and Shipping World,* Feb. 1900, p. 39.
20   Ibid., Sept. 1903, p. 309.
21   Ibid., Aug. 1904, p. 271, July 1904, pp. 243 and 245, Aug. 1904, p. 271.
22   PAC, RG30 CNR records, Vol. 9964, file 3315-11, plan CPR Ottawa West roundhouse, dated 13 March 1925; *Canadian Railway and Marine World,* April 1936, p. 152 and May 1936, p. 210; PAC, RG30, Vol. 7553, file 6-1, letter 10 March 1933.

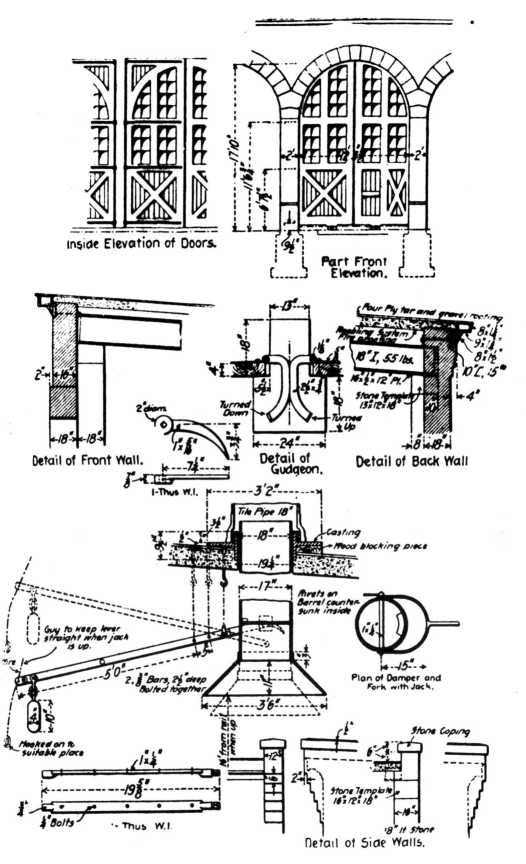

Draftsman's drawings of CPR fireproofing measures, 1902.   – NAC, National Library

The CPR roundhouse at MacTier, Ontario, constructed c.1905. — H.A. Lemkay collection

In retrospect, perhaps the principal feature of CPR roundhouses during this pre-1920 period were the fireproofing measures. The company seems to have kept up with the times, as well, in the introduction of hot-air heating and reinforced-concrete building technique.

The GTR. Turning from the CPR to its principal rival, the Grand Trunk, in the fall of 1904 the London, Ontario, contractor J. Hayman and Sons had under construction a 40-stall roundhouse located in East London, served by a 70-foot pneumatic turntable. The walls were of plain concrete and the roofing was of felt and gravel, which was prevalent on Canadian roundhouses throughout the steam era. An annexed machine shop, 52 feet in width by 112 in length, handled running repairs. From the inner to the outer wall was 80 feet. Steam heat, utilizing condensed steam from a compressor driven by a stationary engine, was pumped through a superheater to what was known as a hot well, thence through heating coils round the building and returning to the hot well. The advantage claimed for the system was the elimination of live steam in the interests of safety. This was common in GTR roundhouses of the time. There is insufficient description to indicate whether this roundhouse was fireproof. A 38-stall roundhouse, with plain concrete walls and roof of wood frame, extant in London, Ontario, according to the Report of the Locomotive and Car Department in 1919 may have been a separate structure, but there is enough similarity in the descriptions from the sources cited to regard these structures as likely one and the same. On the face of it, it is unlikely the GTR would have built two large roundhouses of similar design in the same locality. The floors were for the most part concrete, with parts wood or laid with cinders. An annexed machine shop (47 by 141 feet) and boiler room completed the structure, centred on a 70-foot pneumatic turntable. The office, lunchroom and bunkhouse were housed in adjacent buildings. The steam heating was similar to the previously described structure in East London. The roundhouse was equipped with one drop pit and an air hoist.[23]

The GTR Mimico, Ontario, roundhouse, located a few miles to the west of Toronto, was completed in August 1905. It had a 30-stall capacity, each stall 82 feet in length. The Mimico roundhouse made considerable use of reinforced-concrete construction; the concrete walls were reinforced with trussed bars, and girders and beams were likewise of reinforced concrete, the whole structure being designed on a monolithic principle whereby stress at any particular point was distributed evenly to adjacent panels or members. The roof columns on the inner circle, at the stall entrances, were so designed that if struck inadvertently by a locomotive, they would shift off their foundations but would not break. For the period, the Mimico GTR roundhouse appears to have been of a progressive design. It is, of course, long gone.[24]

The Turcot roundhouse at Montreal, which opened in December 1905, is believed to be extant although not in use. Situated at the foot of a low bluff adjacent to the GTR yards in Lachine, this roundhouse, with its several extensions, was the largest in Canada. An idea of its once intensive activity is conveyed in the well-known photo taken by the CNR in the 1930s. *Railway and Shipping World*, authoritative journal though it undoubtedly was, offers two dates for the opening of the roundhouse, the end of 1905 and close of 1906. According to the November 1908 issue, 40 stalls, 85 feet in length, served by a 100-foot turntable, were opened at the end of 1906. A 17-stall extension of reinforced concrete was added. The roof was wood frame, a construction not favoured by the more progressive engine-house architects of the day because of the fire hazard. The floor was partly concrete and partly cinders. A track led from the roundhouse into the annexed machine shop, which measured 153 by 45 feet, with attached shed for the storage of charcoal, and a wheel and brick shed. The concrete

23 PAC, RG36 series 35 Vol. 23, Report of the Locomotive and Car Department, GTR 1919, pp. 143-5; *Railway and Shipping World*, Sept. 1904, pp. 319 and 321.
24 Ibid., Aug. 1905, p. 363.

Montreal CNR Turcot roundhouse in the 1930s.

machine shop included a smith's shop and attached boiler room. Steam heat and electric light were provided. There were two drop pits for the removal of locomotive wheels, one equipped with a pneumatic jack and the other with a hydraulic. Progressive features in the design of the Turcot roundhouse at the time it was built included the use of reinforced concrete and the provision of electric light, not to mention telephones. The Turcot roundhouse provided the best of terminal care and carried out both light and heavy running repairs. The casting shed, steam-fitter's stores, blacksmith's and carpenter's shop were in adjacent buildings. The Grand Trunk's Turcot roundhouse was undoubtedly the busiest on the system, as on the subsequent CNR's, and probably the busiest in the whole of Canada.[25]

Mention has been made of the Ottawa West CPR roundhouse, built in 1911 and shared with the CNR from 1933. The construction date of the Ottawa CNR roundhouse is unknown, but it may be inferred that it was older than the Ottawa West structure and so built prior to 1911. Its walls were of wood lined with brick. It numbered 22 stalls for the accommodation of locomotives and 6 for use as a tender shop, where repairs were made to cisterns, frames and tender trucks. There were three drop pits, with the machine shop annex opening on two stalls, one of which was used as the blacksmith's shop. The plan drawing, revised in 1933, shows the boiler house and stores building as separate but nearby structures. Heating was by hot air, at least by 1919, according to the GTR report of that year. With its plank flooring the Ottawa GTR roundhouse does not seem to have been to the fore in roundhouse design, but its location, only one mile from Union Station and slightly over that from the Bank Street freight yards, gave it an advantage over the CPR Ottawa West facility. No doubt the old GTR's proximity to the freight yards led to its restriction to yard engines when the two companies pooled their facilities.[26]

In 1912, according to a retired railroader, the GTR opened a concrete 42-stall round-house at Belleville, Ontario, a divisional point on the Montreal-Toronto main line. An aerial photograph taken in 1964 shows a remnant of the original structure, in which the demolished stalls show up in stark clarity. The author has no documentary evidence for the date of construction and so the date 1912 is advanced tentatively, but in any case, the Belleville roundhouse was extant in 1919, the date of the GTR Locomotive and Car Department Report. The stalls were all 90 feet long, 40 stalls were used to accommodate locomotives, one for an air brake and engineer's equipment room, and one to house a steam wrecker. Heating was hot air, and the 80-foot turntable, along with the jacks, was air powered. The annexed machine shop (208 by 48 feet), also of concrete construction, included a smith's shop and tool room, while the air-brake shop was housed in one stall of the roundhouse.[27]

In June 1913 the GTR had under construction a 27-stall roundhouse, at St. Lambert, Quebec, to house the largest locomotives then on the road. The contractor was John S. Metcalf Company, Montreal. The concrete foundations, 2½ feet thick, were carried to bedrock 2½ feet below grade. Construction was of reinforced concrete, brick and timber. The concrete engine pits were 66 feet in length, and four of the stalls were equipped with drop pits. Windows, three per stall along the outer wall, were 14 feet high by 11 wide. Like several of the roundhouses already described, the St. Lambert structure was heated by hot air drawn through steam coils and circulated through ducts by rotary fan 12 feet in diameter. Telescopic jacks over each stall allowed hoods to fit snugly over the stack of any locomotive. The machine shop annex (50 by 155 feet) was of similar construction to the roundhouse,

25 *Railway and Marine World,* Nov. 1908, p. 775; PAC, RG30M, deposit 24, item 717; PAC, RG36 Series 35, Boards, Offices and Commissions, Vol. 23, Report of the Locomotive and Car Department of the Grand Trunk Railway System 1919, pp. 53-7 *passim.*
26 Ibid., pp. 64-7; PAC, RG30 Vol. 7553, file 6-1, letter dated 10 March 1933.
27 PAC. RG36 Series 35, Vol. 23, Report of the Locomotive and Car Department GTR 1919, pp. 79-84.

Layout plan of the Ottawa CNR roundhouse, 1933.

– NAC

Aerial view of Belleville CNR roundhouse in 1964.   – J. Norman Lowe, private collection

An unidentified Grand Trunk Pacific roundhouse and turntable pit under construction in Manitoba, c.1915.
                                                                    – Manitoba Archives

The finishing touches are still being applied to this Grand Trunk Pacific roundhouse in Manitoba, c.1915.
                                                                    – Manitoba Archives

with a track from the same running the full length of the shop. Two 200-horsepower boilers raised steam for heating and auxiliary power. Coal was fed to bunkers in the boiler room by means of hopper chutes filled from gondola cars riding up an inclined track. The turntable, 85 feet long and air powered, was supplied by Dominion Bridge. There is no further information as to when the St. Lambert engine house actually opened, nor when it was finally demolished.[28]

Before leaving the GTR, mention should be made of four roundhouses built by Winnipeg contractor Carter-Halls Aldinger Company for the Grand Trunk Pacific, a short-lived subsidiary of the Grand Trunk. The four locations were Prince George, Endako, Smithers and Pacific, British Columbia, and the cost for the four projects varied between $58,000 and $63,500, to be commenced by 1 June 1915. The specifications called for brick walls, concrete floors, posts, bracing and roof beams of Douglas fir, and tar and gravel roofing. The engine pits were of concrete with timber coping. Beams, trusses and plates were to be of structural steel.[29]

The ICR (Intercolonial Railway). Rhodes, Curry and Company took a contract with the ICR to build a 6-stall (later expanded to 18-stall) roundhouse at Sydney, Nova Scotia), in October 1900, at a total cost of $38,227. The walls, in course of erection by midsummer 1902, were brick, the floor concrete, the roof columns and girders iron. The rubble for the foundations was to be made up of 1 part cement, $2\frac{1}{2}$ parts sand and 5 parts broken stone. Piles were to be of 10-inch spruce. The stalls were 75 feet in length. Steam heat was provided (superseded by hot air in the most up-to-date heating systems) from a nearby boiler house equipped with two 100-horsepower boilers, and a neighbouring building housed the office, storeroom, and engine crews' rooms. The Sydney roundhouse, built in the very early years of the century, impresses one with being of fairly progressive design, although it is unlikely that it was entirely fireproof and it adhered to direct-steam heat.[30]

Late in 1904 the ICR invited tenders for a 30-stall roundhouse at Truro, Nova Scotia, similar in design to roundhouses built or being built at Saint John, New Brunswick, and St. Flavie, Rivière du Loup and Chaudière Junction, Quebec, indicative that it may be considered a standardized ICR design. Construction was brick on stone foundations, with pine used for roof posts, wall beams and piers. The whole structure was divided into five sections by firewalls, a commendable safety feature, but it is doubtful from the brief description that the roof was fireproof. The stalls were 85 feet in length and the engine pits 60 feet. There were two annexes onto the roundhouse proper: one measuring 54 by 115 feet housed the machine shop, boiler and compressor rooms, and coal shed; the other the heating plant, consisting of the circulating fan and engine, and steam coils for the heating of the air, which was then driven by underground conduits into the engine pits. The floor was concrete, and the roofing the standard pitch and gravel. The smoke jacks were cast-iron and adjustable. For its time the Truro roundhouse may be considered a fairly modern one, with both hot-air heating and a considerable measure of fireproofing, although as stated, there is insufficient detail to consider this 1904 structure as completely fireproof.[31]

A 28-stall engine house was completed at Campbellton, New Brunswick, in January 1911. The foundations and engine pits were concrete, and the walls brick, 8 inches thick. The roof was 2-by-4 spruce, laid on edge, supported by wooden columns set in cast-iron shoes on concrete footings. The turntable was 75 feet in length, driven by compressed air. Line drawings of the Campbellton roundhouse, in plan and profile indicate that two of the 85-foot

28 *Canadian Railway and Marine World,* June 1913, pp. 253-4.
29 PAC. RG30, Vol. 11615, file C229; Ibid., Vol. 3990, file 236.
30 *Railway and Shipping World,* June 1902, p. 192; PAC. RG2 Series 1, 30 May 1901, No. 1064-1064a.
31 *Railway and Shipping World,* Dec. 1904, p. 427.

stalls were occupied by the machine shop, engine crews' room and foreman's office, whereas the boiler house, housing three 100-horsepower boilers, was a separate rectangular building connected to the roundhouse by a short passage. The 100-foot chimney rose from a square structure adjacent to the boiler house, connected by underground flue. (The chimney was 54 inches square in its inner dimensions.) Since Campbellton was a major divisional point, the machine shop was well equipped: two forges, drill, grinder, bolt cutter, bolt threader, lathe and shaper. Heating was by hot air, a 30-by-20-foot annex on the other side of the engine house housing the fan and heater, from which hot air was driven through the main duct to the inner face of the structure, from whence it was circulated in a duct around the inner circle, and from there in terra cotta pipes to individual engine pits. A storage room for heavy parts was located on an upper floor above the foreman's office and crew room, with a powered hoist connecting thereto. An industrial track ran round the outer perimeter, with turntable opposite the drop pits (numbers 3, 4 and 5 on the plan) by means of which wheels could be manhandled out of the stalls and along the perimeter track to the machine shop, where another turntable gave access thereto. Not surprisingly, by this date the Campbellton roundhouse was wired for electric light. Overall the engine house, located as it was at a major divisional point, seems to have been reasonably up-to-date by the standards of the time, especially its heating system.[32]

The Charlottetown roundhouse, built in 1910 for the Prince Edward Island Railway, is among the nation's older extant roundhouses. The foundations were concrete, set on concrete piles. There were 20 stalls (our source does not specify their length, but gives the dimensions of the engine pits as 52 feet in length by 3 in width). The roof sloped from 17 feet at the outer, or back, wall to 21 feet at the stall entrance at the front of the roundhouse. The roof was built of grooved spruce planks overlaid with tar and gravel. Direct-steam heat and electric light were provided.[33]

A 3-stall fan-shaped roundhouse, no longer extant, was built in Summerside, Prince Edward Island, in 1906. This incipient type of roundhouse was the most common across Canada, located at countless minor divisional points and branch line terminals, such as Summerside. It was constructed principally of spruce and pine, fireproofing being of much less concern in an engine house of this size, which could be evacuated fairly quickly. The exterior seems to have been shingled. The stalls were 62 feet in length and the engine pits 45 feet. The roof had a slight slope, as can be seen on the plan, from the front wall slightly over 18 feet in height to the back wall a little under 15 feet. There were six windows on the back wall and three on the side walls. The roof was tongue-and-groove spruce covered with 5-ply pitch and gravel. The doors were tongue-and-groove pine. There are no details available on heating and lighting.[34]

One may surmise from the foregoing that ICR roundhouses were abreast of developments, if not in the vanguard. A dearth of illustrations precludes any conclusions or generalizations as to distinctive style in Intercolonial roundhouses. Obviously the ICR had a standardized roundhouse. These roundhouses of similar design were built at a number of points in the early years of the century.

The CNoR (Canadian Northern). Begun as a prairie road by William Mackenzie and Donald Mann in the late 1880s, the Canadian Northern was incorporated by federal statute in 1899. In little more than a decade it became Canada's second transcontinental railway. As early as the spring of 1901 the CNoR claimed to have recently built a fireproof roundhouse,

32 *Railway and Marine World,* July 1911, pp. 637 and 639.
33 PAC. RG30M deposit 22, item 126.
34 PAC. RG30M deposit 22, item 126.

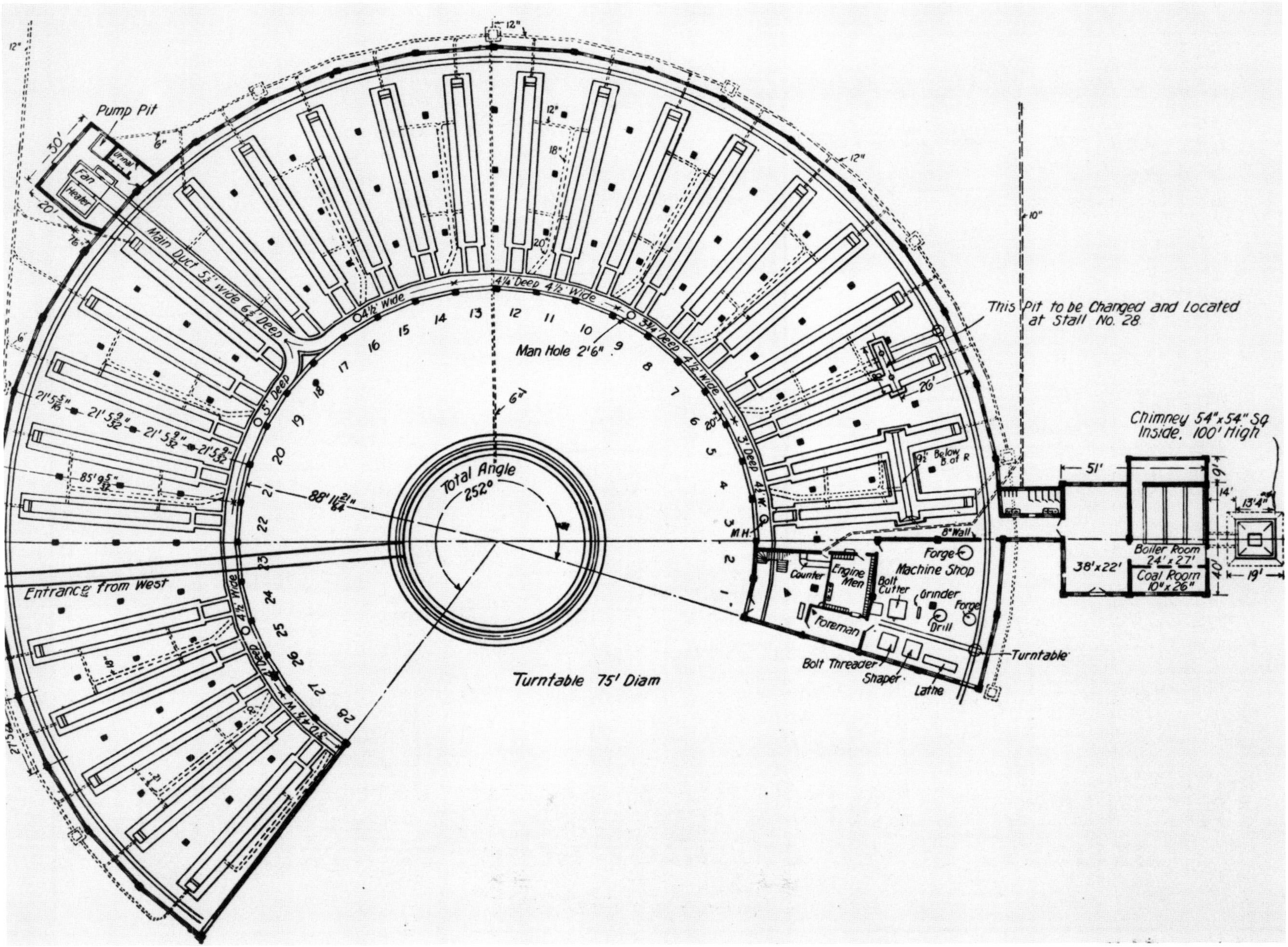

Chimney 54"x54" Sq. Inside. 100' High

This Pit to be Changed and Located at Stall No. 28

Boiler Room 24' x 27'

Coal Room 10' x 26'

38' x 22'

Forge
Machine Shop
Bolt Cutter
Engine Men
Counter
Foreman
Drill Grinder
Forge
Bolt Threader
Shaper
Lathe
Turntable

Turntable 75' Diam

Total Angle 252°

Man Hole 2'6"

Main Duct 5½' wide 6⅓' Deep

Entrance from West

Pump Pit
Fan
Heater

Draftsman's plan of the ICR Campbellton, New Brunswick, roundhouse, 1911. — *Railway & Marine World*, July 1911, p. 637

69

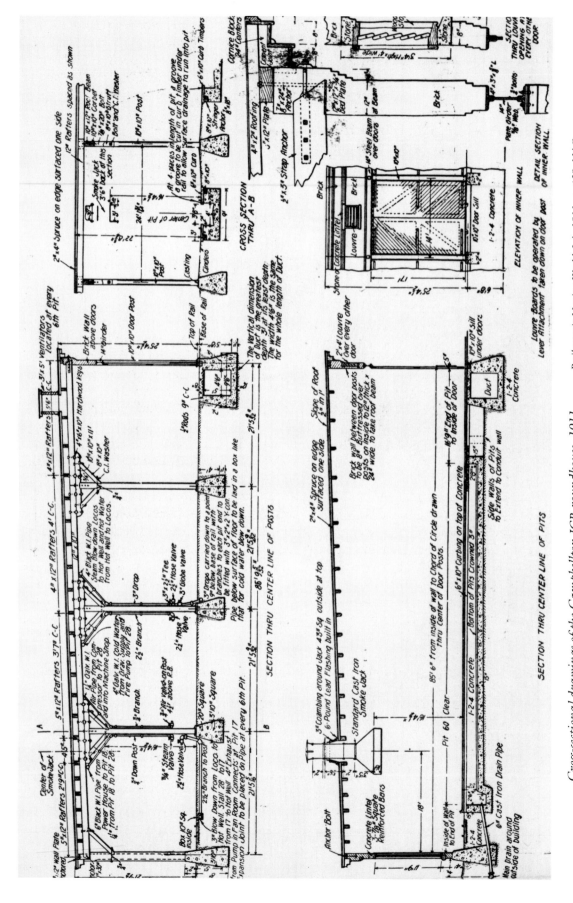

Cross-sectional drawings of the Campbellton ICR roundhouse, 1911. — *Railway & Marine World*, July 1911, p. 639, NAC

without however giving the location. Their assertion was based on the use of a new construction material made of "expanded metal lathe and cement," in the words of *Railway and Shipping World*. The material was said to be cheaper than brick or stone and was comprised of light steel studding, to which lathe was securely wired, then plaster applied to both sides, forming a wall 2 to $2\frac{1}{2}$ inches thick — strong, rigid, non-conductive and fireproof. Whether this construction, bound together by Portland cement, was a patented process is unknown.[35]

By at least 1906 the Canadian Northern had produced a standard engine house design. Draftsman's drawings give the impression of structures boasting some architectural distinction, in the manner of the early CPR roundhouses. The use of grouped windows with a number of lights, set with lintels and sills, suggests a symmetry of almost classic lines in these utilitarian structures. An example of one of this series of CNoR roundhouses was built in Toronto (Cherry Street and Eastern Avenue) in 1908-09 as a 7-stall fan-shaped structure. A rectangular annex ran diagonally off one side, comprising the machine shop, blacksmith's shop, boiler room, office, stores, coal shed and washrooms. The stalls were about 83 feet in length, $13\frac{1}{2}$ feet wide at the entrance, and extended to $25\frac{1}{2}$ feet along the back wall, or perimeter. The walls were 9-inch brick on a concrete foundation, and the floors were also concrete. The roofing was the conventional felt, tar and gravel. (There is no mention of the metal lath and cement process.) The ceiling beams and purlins were of wood, as were the roof posts. There were five pairs of windows along the two side walls and three per stall along the rear wall for a total of 21. The stone window sills and lintel set the windows off in an aesthetically pleasing fashion; in 1908 roundhouses had not yet become completely plain and utilitarian structures. Referring to the front elevation of the roundhouse, note the stall doors, without glazing, and the transom lights running along the front wall just below the roof line. With its brick walls and stone facings, the Toronto roundhouse, when first constructed, must have been a rather handsome structure.[36]

In 1911 the CNoR prepared plans for a 15-stall roundhouse at Trenton, Ontario, probably built the following year. This is of particular interest because a former Canadian National roundhouse survives in Trenton today, although half of it has been demolished. The Trenton roundhouse is no longer in railway use but has been sold or leased to a commercial enterprise, Trenton Glass and Window Ltd., and so serves a very different function from what it once did. When the author visited the structure, the walls gave the appearance of concrete or cement block. This surviving structure has not been positively identified with the CNoR construction of about 1912, but such an origin is likely. The brief description available, to be found in the CNR inventory of 1919, describes the engine house as a concrete structure, which tallies with the appearance of the surviving building. There were two 9-inch brick firewalls. Most of the floor was cinders, but three of the stalls, reserved for boiler wash-out purposes, were floored with concrete. The stalls were 90 feet in length and the engine pits 58 feet, with drop pits in two of the stalls. A narrow-gauge perimeter track ran round the back wall, connecting with the drop pits and machine shop by small turntables. The 60-by-100-foot machine shop was floored with cement and the roof supported by five steel trusses. There were, according to the plan, three boilers, but whether the roundhouse was steam or hot-air heated is not known.[37]

The first 12 stalls of the Regina, Saskatchewan, roundhouse were built in 1912 and subsequently added to in 1919 and 1922, numbering 24 in the latter year. Those built in 1912 were 87 feet in length, those added in 1919 were $91\frac{1}{2}$ feet, and the last six to complete

---

35 *Railway and Shipping World*, April 1901, p. 104.
36 PAC. RG30M, access. 78903/42, item 665; Ibid., item 663; Ibid., item 667.
37 Canadian Northern Railway Co., Encyclopaedia CNR, (Montreal, 1918), PAC, RG30M, deposit 24, item 313.

Plan of CNoR roundhouse, Toronto, 1908.

– NAC, National Map Collection

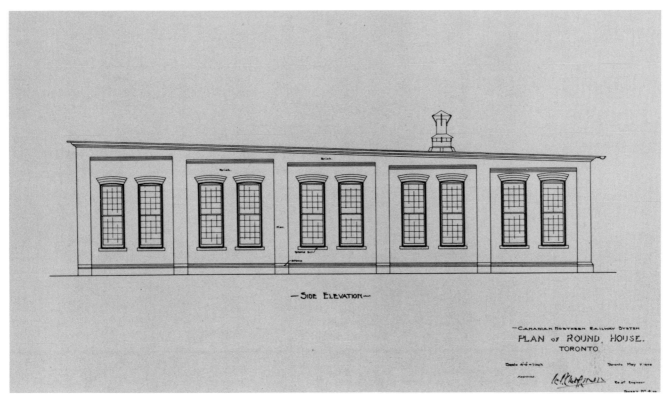

Profile drawing of the CNoR roundhouse, Toronto, 7 May 1908.   – NAC, National Map Collection

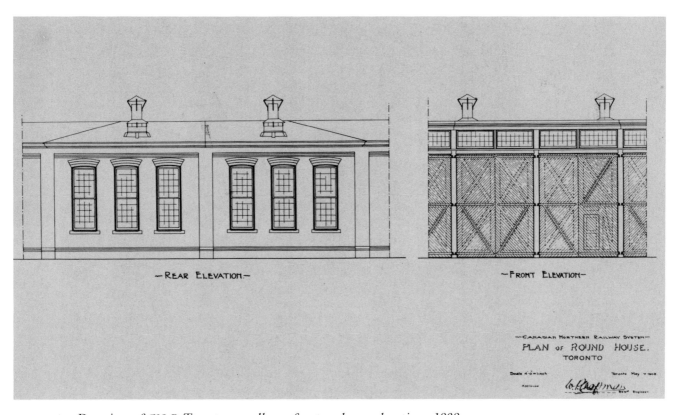

Drawings of CNoR Toronto roundhouse front and rear elevations, 1908.
– NAC, National Map Collection

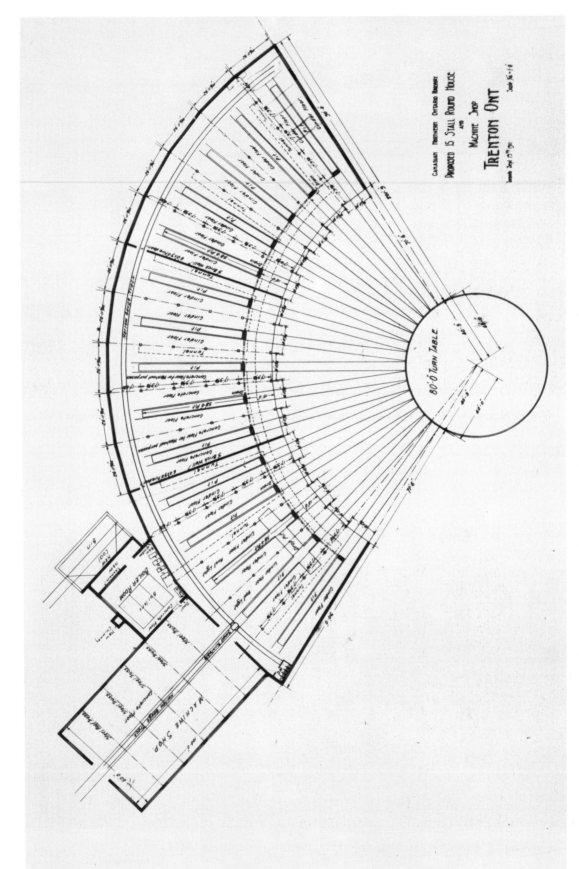

Plan drawing of Trenton, Ontario, roundhouse, CNR 1911.

– NAC, National Map Collection

Rear view of the CNR roundhouse at Kamsask, Saskatchewan.   – Manitoba Archives

Canadian Northern roundhouse at Kipling, Saskatchewan.   – Manitoba Archives

the structure in 1922 were slightly short of 101 feet. As finally completed, or perhaps as early as 1912 considering the significance of the location, a 50-by-125 foot machine shop, boiler room, and the usual facilities were part of the structure. The significant point about the former CNoR roundhouse at Regina is that it is one of the extant structures presently in use by the CNR line serving the terminal.[38]

The CNoR drew up plans for a small 3-stall segmental engine house at Sudbury, Ontario, to which the Canadian Northern ran a spur line from its main divisional point at Capreol in May 1908. Construction seems similar to the one in Toronto, previously described in some detail, with 9-inch brick walls, in which were set windows 20 feet high with stone sills and probably stone lintels. The foundations were of concrete, as were the engine pits. The roof was covered with tongue-and-groove sheathing, as were the outside of the 16-by-6-foot doors.[39]

The Canadian Northern Quebec Railway was incorporated in 1906 and ownership was transferred to the Canadian Northern in 1914. A plan dated 28 November 1911 shows in side elevation the CNQR proposed roundhouse at Quebec City, probably built the following year. The 15-stall roundhouse centred on a 75-foot turntable. The foundations were concrete, as were the 12-inch-thick walls. An important feature was the provision of two fire walls, with fire doors, but the roof and its supporting members were probably of wood. The roofing was the standard felt, tar and gravel, used on most railways with few exceptions at this time. The fire walls divided the house into three segments and one had a concrete floor, but the other two were cinder. A perimeter track gave access to the machine shop. Another significant feature in the design was the provision of asbestos smoke jacks. The stalls were 92 feet in length and the engine pits 58 feet. On the side walls there were five spacious windows, 13 feet 7 inches in height by 10 feet 2 inches in breadth, and presumably windows of similar dimensions along the back wall at each stall. The wooden doors were surmounted by rectangular transoms. Finally, there was a tunnel round the inner circumference, the purpose for which is unknown. No further details have been found on this Quebec City roundhouse, nor any others on the CNQR.[40]

The NTR (National Transcontinental Railway). Completed on 17 November 1913 from Moncton, New Brunswick, to Winnipeg, Manitoba, this government-built line was constructed to very high specifications and at considerable cost. Traversing the hitherto uninhabited regions of Quebec and Ontario on a direct route from Quebec City to Winnipeg, the NTR spanned a region with as severe climatic conditions as any along the route of the three transcontinentals. For this reason one would expect to find solidly built facilities, and this seems to be the case with the roundhouses.

At the outset a standard roundhouse based on designs furnished by the Grand Trunk Pacific was adopted: 12-stall, set on concrete foundations to 4 feet above grade, the walls thereon being of red brick. The roof was carried on wooden columns (probably Douglas fir), wooden girders and beams. Steel columns were used at the entrance to the stalls, along the inner circle. Obviously such a structure would not be fireproof. According to one account in *Railway and Marine World*, the annexes comprising the machine shop and boiler room were grouped at one end to leave the other open for expansion, but in another context it was

---

38 Engineer's Office, CNR Regional Office, Winnipeg, plan 120-110, sheet 14. The Regina yardmaster's office informs us that the yards are soon to be relocated, with the likelihood that the roundhouse will be demolished. The Regina CN roundhouse is one of the original CNoR standard designs, described in the text. Together with the CN roundhouse at Prince Albert, Sask., these are the sole survivors of the one time Canadian Northern Railway standard roundhouse.

39 PAC, RG30M, National Map Coll., accession 78903/42, item 616, 617.

40 Ibid., access. 81203/8, item 3, item 2, CNR Inventory, Section F8.

reported that these facilities were to be housed in adjacent structures. The company's round-houses were to be 91 feet in depth between inner and outer walls, with engine pits 60 feet in length, concrete throughout, with timber sills. Turntables were to be 75½ feet in length and rails were to be 80 pounds. The floors were to be laid in cinders to a depth of 4 inches, except for wood planking to serve as a walkway the length of the engine pit. An industrial track of 2-foot gauge ran around the inner wall, with turntables for transference of wheels from the drop pit to the machine shop. The machine shop annex was to be 56½ feet by 112 feet, and next to this the boiler room and engine room. The engine room, 48 by 43 feet, housed the heating plant, air compressors and washing plant, and the 29-by-43-foot boiler room housed two boilers. The whole structure was electrically lit. Such was the general layout for the company's roundhouses.[41] In all, 16 roundhouses of this design were built for the National Transcontinental along the 1,800-mile route from Moncton to Winnipeg, all but two of which were of 12-stall capacity, while the one at Graham, Ontario, had 18 stalls and one at Transcona (Winnipeg) had 24 stalls. Machine shop annexes were included at Moncton, Napadogan, Edmunston, Parent, Cochrane, Grant and Graham. The published *Report of the National Transcontinental Railway Investigatory Commission* (1914) found that the costs for these structures were grossly excessive, running as high as 33 percent above those of equivalent roundhouses built by the CPR along the north shore of Lake Superior, a region climatically akin to the more northerly route of the NTR. These costs were attributed to the method of awarding contracts and to building them to the full 12-stall size shown on the plans, regardless of whether anywhere near that number were needed at the outset. The Commission found that a proper interpretation of the contract indicated that building roundhouses was not part of the government's obligation in the first place. Presumably the roundhouses were well built, of brick on concrete foundations, but in any case, they were expensive. According to the Appendix A listing of extant roundhouses on the CNR, only those at Edmunston, New Brunswick and Transcona (Winnipeg) have survived to the present.

Some detail is available on the NTR roundhouse opened in 1913 at O'Brien, Quebec, 113 miles east of Cochrane, Ontario, in the dismal bush-covered terrain of the clay belt. The O'Brien roundhouse was built by the Montreal concern of F. Munro and Company, probably under subcontract, for $59,189.44, which was exclusive of the machine shop and the heating apparatus. The structure, following the general specifications for the NTR, was brick walled on concrete foundations. The roofs of the machine shop, boiler and engine rooms were supported on steel trusses, and there were skylights over the drop pits and machine shop. There were 12 stalls, exactly 91 feet in length. The machine shop, boiler room and engine room, whether annexes or separate buildings, were rectangular in shape. There were smoke jacks over each engine pit. The roof was guaranteed for ten years and was made up of 5-ply felt, each of which was secured by pitch and tar, and the whole covered with one-half inch of gravel.[42]

All wood for heavy framing was British Columbia fir or yellow pine, and door and window frames were of white pine. The stall doors were white pine hung on steel columns. Flooring was of 3-inch plank spiked to 4-by-6-inch sleepers laid on gravel, except in the engine room and machine shop, where the wooden flooring had a concrete base. All interior brickwork was painted with two coats of whitewash, and iron and sheet metal painted black. All woodwork had one coat of primer and two of white lead and linseed oil. The glazing for the skylights and engine room doors was ¼-inch-thick wire glass. All plumbing was of heavy cast iron. The whole roundhouse was wired for 110-volt lamps; inside the roundhouse were 12

---

41   *Canadian Railway and Marine World*, Nov. 1913, pp. 511-2.
42   PAC, RG2, Series 1, Privy Council records, 23 May 1913, No. 1230.

arc lamp outlets, with two more at the front of the roundhouse, all of which were controlled by inside switches. The hot-air heating system was based on exhaust steam supplied at atmospheric pressure to the heater coils. The system was designed to maintain a temperature of 60 degrees Fahrenheit with the outside temperature at minus 20 degrees.[43]

The only photograph found of an NTR roundhouse was of the one at Cochrane. There is no documentary material, but the construction was similar to the one already described at O'Brien, since the NTR had standardized the design. The Cochrane roundhouse originally had 12 stalls but judging from the number of smoke jacks, the structure had been expanded to 17 or 18 stalls. Cochrane was a major divisional point between Quebec City and Winnipeg, and a machine shop was included in the design of its roundhouses. The boiler house annex appears at the far end of the roundhouse, as laid down in the general specifications. There were three windows in each of the side walls. The neighbouring two-storey house with verandah served as the foreman's office and bunkhouse. This roundhouse has been demolished and its T&NO neighbour burned down.

The T&NO (Temiskaming & Northern Ontario Railway). Incorporated under a provincial commission in 1902, the T&NO was built to tap the mining district of northern Ontario.

In a comparatively short regional railway such as the T&NO (North Bay to Timmins and Kirkland Lake, with extension to Cochrane and Moosonee), all within one climatic region, one would not expect variations in design except over a period of time. Hence, in describing one of the early T&NO roundhouses, perhaps we have described them all. The 8-stall-capacity Cochrane roundhouse, completed in 1910 of reinforced-concrete construction on concrete foundations was built by the Forest Paving Company. It must be credited with a quite progressive design for that period, having a roof of reinforced-concrete slabs supported by steel roof trusses. Annexed was a machine shop of square configuration (52 by 54 feet) and an erecting room, equipped with a 10-ton travelling crane, indicating that very extensive shop work was carried out here. A list of the machine shop equipment will be found in the notes. The Cochrane roundhouse was taken out of service at the end of January 1959 and sold to Cochrane Industries Ltd., a manufacturer of plywood, in 1962. According to local report, the roundhouse was destroyed by fire about that time and the present plant erected on the foundations. How this could have been so, given the construction, is beyond the author's ability to explain, for concrete does not burn well. Whatever the case, the present configuration of walls and ceilings is unmistakably that of a roundhouse, although the exterior bears little resemblance to one.[44]

Until 1908 the T&NO shared the CPR roundhouse at North Bay (only the machine shop of the latter structure has survived). In 1908 the T&NO opened its own roundhouse at North Bay, which was its principal terminal and then as now the home of its head office. This engine house was contracted to Forest City Paving Company, which also had the contract for the one at Englehart and perhaps for all the roundhouses the length of the line. When first built, the North Bay roundhouse could accommodate 15 locomotives, and there was a machine shop annex (85 by 52 feet) with adjoining tinsmith's and welding shop. The original stalls were 90 feet in length, but in 1925 six more of 100 feet were added, in which columns and girders were of reinforced steel. At this date the concrete floors were topped by wood blocks.

---

43 Ibid.
44 *Ninth Annual Report of the Temiskaming and Northern Ontario Railway Commission* 1910, (Toronto: King's Printer, 1911), pp. 74-5; J. Norman Lowe, "New Uses for Roundhouses," *Canadian Transportation*, June 1964, p. 26; Engineer's Office, Ontario Northlands Railway, North Bay, O., reference cards; *Eighth Annual Report* T&NO *Railway Commission 1909*, (Toronto: King's Printer, 1910), p. 17.

NTR roundhouse, Cochrane, Ontario, 1915.

– J. Norman Lowe, private collection

There were three boilers, for each of which there was a 64-foot smokestack 28 inches in diameter. Six stalls were demolished in 1963, the rest taken down at some subsequent date.[45]

Forest City Paving put up the Englehart roundhouse in 1908. This had a concrete roof. A 6-stall extension dating from 1925 featured columns and roof girders of structural steel encased in concrete, but the roof purlins and sheathing were of wood. The 6-stall extension was undertaken by the Britnell Construction Company, Toronto. The floor was wood blocks laid on concrete. The Englehart roundhouse was retired on 9 November 1972.[46]

The PGE (Pacific Great Eastern Railway, subsequently British Columbia Railway). This pre-1920 section closes with a brief look at the roundhouses on the Pacific Great Eastern Railway, along which may be seen constructions of more modest and conservative design, with economy in mind. The PGE was incorporated by provincial statute to build north from Vancouver, through the interior of British Columbia, to reach the Grand Trunk Pacific, as it then was, at Fort George. The first roundhouse built by the PGE in 1914 was at Squamish, which for may years remained the southern terminal. The 6-stall Squamish roundhouse was of timber construction with concrete floor and pits. A machine shop was annexed. The 75-foot steel turntable was manually operated. The stalls were 87 feet in length, and one was equipped with a drop pit. The roof sloped gently from a height of 22 feet at the front to 18 at the back.[47]

Summary

To sum up, during the early years of this century, the principal advances in roundhouse design in Canada were the use of reinforced concrete, steel roof trusses and the fireproof roundhouse. Hot-air or hot-blast heat was also significant, and it goes almost without saying that the introduction of electric light was too.

---

45 Engineer's Office, ONR North Bay, records; J. Norman Lowe, *Canadian National in the East*, Vol. 1, p. 4; Engineer's Office, ONR North Bay, records, file 1835-11, 1835-5; *Fourteenth Annual Report* T&NO *Railway Commission 1915*, (Toronto: King's Printer, 1916), p. 61.
46 Engineer's Office, ONR North Bay, file 1935-6.
47 British Columbia Railway, Pacific Great Eastern Railway Co. — history & data; BCR records, plan Squamish roundhouse, PGE.

THE ROUNDHOUSE IN THE ERA OF BIG POWER 1920-50

The post-WWI years to mid-century, commonly referred to by railroaders as the era of Big Power, saw the development of the steam locomotive in North America to unprecedented dimensions. Nowhere else in the world did Big Power reach the size that it did on American roads. Engine houses had to accommodate the monsters which successively replaced the smaller engines, engines which had seemed big when the century was young. Although Canadian manifestation of these changes was somewhat less dramatic than in America the same forces were at work, and if Canadian locomotives overall were smaller than their American counterparts, they were still bigger than most others elsewhere in the world.

The years between the world wars saw further development of fireproofing techniques, increased use of the electric hoist, improvement in hot-air heating, and continued advances in structural design. Roundhouses had perforce to increase in size to accommodate the much larger locomotives. Sometimes this was done by stall extensions through the back wall, but as often by demolition and construction of a new facility. Much of the change in this period involved development and refinement of techniques or designs introduced earlier in the century, or in some instances the 1890s, such as roof trusses and hot-air or hot-blast heating. Reinforced concrete was increasingly used, particularly for roof posts, girders, beams and purlins. Perhaps the most signal innovation was one of engine handling technique, rather than architectural design. This was direct steaming, which was first seen in Canada in 1929, speeding up engine turnaround time. Roundhouse crews were under continual pressure to reduce this to the minimum. Individuality of design merged into utilitarian uniformity, drab but functional, in contrast to the CPR roundhouses of the 1880s or the rather handsome CNoR structures built in the early years of this century.

State of the Art in the 1920s and 1930s

In the November 1919 issue of the Chicago publication *Journal of the Western Society of Engineers*, an article appeared under the signature of Exum M. Haas, engineer consultant with the Austin Company, Cleveland, Ohio. "Modern Tendencies in Roundhouse Design" was an apt title, and one cannot do better than to start with this article in a study of roundhouses for this period.

By 1919 increasing locomotive size, coupled with higher costs, demanded improved roundhouse design. Time studies indicated that a 15-minute cut in servicing each engine for the road would save about $300 per day. Improvement in roundhouse design would make fuller use of each locomotive's earning capacity and would make the roundhouse a less arduous and forbidding place to work. Already, Haas asserted, there was evident a decline in the calibre of men, or the quality of labour, and more congenial workplaces were to be found at equivalent or higher rates of pay. Roundhouses built at the turn of the century were no longer conducive to economical or efficient operation. By 1919, however, the provision of gib and bridge cranes, electric hoists, and improved heating and ventilation were harbingers of both easier and safer working conditions in the future. In this connection Haas advocated the use of reinforced concrete and other non-combustibles in construction. Attention increasingly was paid to roof design, for this remained the vulnerable part of the roundhouse.[48]

Haas described the structural design of American roundhouses under three headings. The most common roundhouses, because the most economical, were built with brick walls, wood frames and wooden roofs. (As will soon be seen, brick walls figured in two of the most advanced Canadian roundhouses of the time, built in Toronto in 1929-30.) In the next

---

48   Exum M. Haas, "Modern Tendencies in Roundhouase Design," *Journal of the Western Society of Engineers,* (Chicago), Nov. 1919, p. 570.

category, Haas placed those with a reinforced-concrete frame and roof, and in the top class those built with a steel frame and reinforced concrete. The fire hazard was ever a factor with those roundhouses employing any amount of wood in their design. Frame roundhouses continued in service throughout the steam era, particularly smaller houses which could be evacuated more quickly in an emergency, but for the larger structures wood was not favoured. As we shall see, wood was rarely eliminated entirely, even in the largest Canadian roundhouses, until very late in the day.

As early as 1919 Haas was able to cite advanced construction designs in the U.S., but it must be noted that these were exceptions rather than the rule. American design was generally more advanced than Canadian by reason of the heavier demands made on the busier American roads. Two examples of American construction techniques in the early post-war period were the Western Maryland Railway's new roundhouse at Hagerstown, Maryland, featuring a steel frame encased in concrete and a double monitor roof, and the Pittsburgh & Lake Erie Railway's new roundhouses, using steel-frame construction and a gypsum roof. The increased use of steel trusses as roof supports reduced the need for roof posts obstructing the interior. Roundhouse roofs, often with monitors, were of increased height in the interests of both light and ventilation. Other improvements cited by Haas were 4 to 5-ply roofs, improved roof drainage, more durable steel sash for windows, a steel-framed stall door, and also an overhead rolling wood-slat door.[49]

Electric hoists and bridge cranes greatly facilitated heavy maintenance work. According to Haas, the first such installation, a product of the Baldwin Locomotive Company, was in 1902 in Philadelphia for the Pennsylvania Railroad. One of the more hazardous operations in the roundhouse had been that at the drop pits, where locomotive wheels were removed for servicing in the machine shop. The electric hoist proved both more efficient and safer than the hydraulic jacks for this operation.[50]

Both heating and ventilation systems underwent progressive improvement. The round-house was by nature a draughty, inadequately heated structure. The hot-blast system was no longer new by the date that Haas wrote, but improved systems were replacing pipe coils and radiators, proving their superiority to direct-steam heat. Once adequate fans had been designed, the hot-air system provided more efficient heat in winter and a ventilation system by use of the fans alone in summer. Likewise, more effective exhaust systems were being devised.[51]

Haas's concept of the modern roundhouse embraced two basic types of structure: what he termed type A, equipped for light running repairs, located at all but important divisional points and terminals; and type B, to handle much heavier work, short of repair and erecting shops. Type A should be designed with a reinforced-concrete frame, concrete beam construction, an insulated roof, with concrete T-beams supporting longitudinal beams, or purlins, following the centre line of the stall; the roof should be designed with monitors to shed plenty of natural light on the work area. Presumably the construction of the type B roundhouse was along the same lines, but the difference lay in its size and equipment. Type B should have both an overhead crane, travelling on a rail 26 feet 6 inches above the floor and spanning about 50 feet, and an electric hoist for the removal of wheels. He recommended a high monitor and large ventilator in conjunction with the smoke jack over each stall; this, with the hot-blast system, should exhaust all gases within the house. He had serious reservations about

---

49   Ibid., p. 574.
50   *Railway Mechanical Engineer,* Sept. 1919, pp. 521-2.
51   Exum M. Haas, op. cit., pp. 578-9.

the use of drop pits and jacks because of their highly hazardous nature, particularly in light of the increased weight of locomotives and the declining quality in roundhouse labour.[52]

The American Railway Association, in its 1928 convention at Atlantic City, New Jersey, stressed the need for fireproof construction insofar as possible, recommending concrete with steel framing and fireproof smoke jacks. On the other hand, reinforced-concrete construction was superior to concrete with steel framing where exposed to exhaust gases. A plain concrete floor was good, but difficult to repair; brick and cinder floors were not recommended. A floor with a concrete base served well topped by a waterproof durable substance which would stand up to heavy trucking. Creosoted yellow pine block laid on a 5-inch concrete base had been tried in 1926 on the Southern Railway by its architect, Hugo W. Hesselbach, and found promising. *Railway Engineering and Maintenance*, in discussing the merits of different types of floor, rated concrete floors as good but noted that they tended to become slippery; vitrified brick was also good but awkward for the trucking of heavy loads. The engineer of buildings on the Chicago, Rock Island & Pacific Railroad expressed a preference for asphalt floors; he contended that wood block floors were too subject to expansion and contraction.[53]

Roofs of reinforced concrete slabs supported by pre-cast roof beams had found favour on the Pennsylvania Railroad as early as 1920, as had floors of creosoted wood blocks on a sand and concrete base. Light weight reinforced-concrete slabs for roofs had been developed by 1924, according to *Railway Engineering and Maintenance*. These slabs were impregnated with air cells to the degree that their weight was reduced by two thirds by comparison with a solid-concrete roof slab. A roof of laminated wood was reported on the Southern Pacific Railway in 1928, reputedly firewood. It consisted of 2-by-4 Douglas fir laid on edge, on which was laid asbestos impregnated with asphalt. The Southern Pacific at this time favoured reinforced-concrete frames and wall panels in the construction of walls, and hung steel doors. By 1929 *Railway Engineering and Maintenance*, on the subject of roundhouse roofing, reported two types in general use in the U.S., pitch and gravel, and asphalt and felt. The first was slightly the more expensive and was the type to be generally found in Canada; the second could be laid on a much steeper slope, required a little more attention, but allegedly could be repaired by one man.[54]

So far construction materials and methods have been described. Now attention is directed to operations within the roundhouse and annexed machine shop. Travelling cranes and electric hoists came into general use in the machine shops required to do the heavier and more involved maintenance. By 1931 the building engineers on both the Illinois Central and the Chicago, Rock Island & Pacific railroads had no doubts as to the superiority of hot-air heat, with the fans and heating units well protected and seldom damaged, whereas the reverse was the case with pipes or radiators. Neither hot water or direct steam could compare with hot air.[55]

The 1920s witnessed two major developments which saved both time and money in roundhouse servicing: one was transference of the ash pit inside the roundhouse, and the other direct steaming. Early in 1923 *Railway Mechanical Engineer* announced that the National Boiler Washing Company, Chicago, had devised a dual-function engine pit for the National Consolidated Locomotive Terminal. The locomotives' fires were pulled inside the roundhouse, the engine pit being designed with a sub-pit for the reception and removal of ashes from the firebox. This eliminated the traditional stop outside at the ash pit and the need

---

52 Ibid., pp. 577-8, 576.
53 *Canadian Railway and Marine World,* Aug. 1928, pp. 458-9.
54 *Railway Age,* Vol. 68, No. 24, 11 June 1920, pp. 1663-64; *Railway and Engineering Maintenance,* May 1928, p. 199; Ibid., July 1929, p. 308.
55 *Railway Engineering and Maintenance,* June 1931, p. 564.

for hostler service. With this system the road crew brought the locomotive into the round-house themselves and picked it up there when ready for the road. The Chicago terminal installation included boiler washing facilities at each stall. The time for the servicing of a locomotive, on a rough average, was reduced from 9 hours 30 minutes to 4 hours 35 minutes by these and kindred operations, not to mention cutting fuel and water costs almost in half at the terminal.[56]

Probably the most significant development in roundhouse operation in the post-war period was direct steaming, resulting in much faster servicing, savings in coal consumption and a virtually smoke-free roundhouse. The concept had been mooted and experimental work done as early as 1885, but direct steaming became a practical proposition only in 1938 on the Grand Trunk Western, as the result of the joint efforts of GTW engineers and the Railway Engineering Company of Chicago. Direct steaming was taken up in Canada by both the CPR and the TH&B within a year or two of its GTW debut.[57]

Direct steaming virtually eliminated the hour or more formerly required to get up steam in preparation for the road. The locomotive was fired up much more quickly by having its boiler connected to a steam line in the roundhouse and the pressure held at 150 pounds. When ready for service it moved out of the roundhouse to the firing-up track under this initial boiler pressure, the operation of filling the boiler with preheated water taking but half an hour. At the firing-up track the coal shovelled into the firebox while still in the roundhouse was ignited by means of a portable fuel-oil torch, a matter of five to six minutes, after which the locomotive was ready for the road. Direct steaming reduced coal consumption by about two-thirds. The elimination of corrosive gases and smoke from the roundhouse meant better working conditions and longer life for the structure itself. All the plant required was two 300-horsepower boilers and power feed to each boiler from the powerhouse.[58]

In the late 1920s the American Railway Association recommended the maximum of window space consistent with sound construction — windows in the rear wall, side walls, doors and transoms at the entrance to the stalls, and monitor-type roofs. By this time lens lights had come into use, whereby light was focused where needed. The Association recommended their installation between each stall and 13 feet above the floor to illuminate the area between the stalls. Each roof post or column should have a 100-watt bulb with reflector on a flexible lead to illuminate the rods and running gear. One or two floodlights were mounted on the inner wall, playing on the tracks at the front of the roundhouse, converging on the turntable and pit. Electrical outlets for welding should be available on roof posts at least at every other stall. Drop pits should be equipped with fixed lights in the walls.

By the mid-1930s the American Railway Engineering Association was emphasizing fire prevention, with the provision of firewalls at 10-stall intervals and the use of non-corrosive and fireproof building materials. Stalls should be at least 20 feet longer than the overall length of the biggest locomotive on the road, including the tender. Ten feet should be allowed between the pilot or cowcatcher and the back wall, for it was at the front end of the locomotive that much of the work was done. Enough space should be left at the front of the stall to detach the tender and still leave room to walk without opening the stall doors. Engine pits should be well drained, at both ends if necessary, and the floor should be convex for this reason. Engine pits should be at least 3 feet 9 inches wide and between 2 feet 6 inches and 3 feet deep. Generally speaking, the roundhouse should be equipped with one drop pit to handle

56 *Railway Mechanical Engineer*, Feb. 1923, pp. 113-6 *passim*.
57 Ibid.
58 *Railway Age*, (East Stroudberg, Penn: Simmons-Boardman) 14 April 1928, pp. 861-3 *passim*.

the very large and heavy driving wheels, and another for the smaller engine truck, trailing and tender wheels.[59]

By 1935 lighting was so designed as to avoid shadows, with an expenditure of 300 to 500 watts per stall, supplemented by outlets for drop-cord lamps and for welding equipment. Outlets were also avail able between the stalls. A variety of mechanical aids was available by this date, such as electrically driven tractors, trucks and portable cranes. Overhead or travelling cranes were, of course, reserved for roundhouses where considerable shop work was done.[60]

Overall one may hazard the opinion that the modern roundhouse, in considering its various components, was in place by the early 1920s, save for direct steaming and some refinements in construction. During this whole period the demands of the locomotive rapidly increased by reason of its very size, for by the 1920s the massive locomotive was the dominant feature in North American railroading. The same factors were at work in Canadian as in American railroading, although in somewhat attenuated form. Lines of development were similar north of the boundary as south of it, as the following pages will indicate, although American progress led the way.

The Canadian Roundhouse in the Era of Big Power 1920 to 1950

In this final phase of the story of the Canadian roundhouse, particular note will be taken of the CPR Toronto roundhouse, the TH&B engine house in Hamilton, Ontario, and the CPR St. Luc roundhouse, Montreal, as exemplifying the latest design and facilities on Canadian roads. With the foregoing description of American trends, it may then be possible to assess Canadian development in the design of the roundhouse and the facilities provided. In this the reader need not anticipate much that is distinctively Canadian. A few structures, such as that at The Pas, Manitoba, are included as being typical of the run-of-the-mill sort of roundhouse to be found across the country at divisional points and minor terminals. In the succeeding pages less stress is laid on company characteristics for two reasons. In the first place, the number of companies was significantly reduced with the nationalization of the Canadian Northern, the Grand Trunk, and the Grand Trunk Pacific railways in the formation of the Canadian National Railways Company. Secondly, as time went on, roundhouses assumed unadorned utilitarian lines in which, at least outwardly, little distinguished the roundhouses on one road from those on another.

Joffre Roundhouse, Quebec. The original Joffre roundhouse, located in the Charny yards about 5 miles west of Lévis on the ICR, was built around the turn of the century and was the busiest divisional point on the system apart from Moncton. To date no information on the original structure has been forthcoming, but late in 1921 a 15-stall addition brought the total capacity of the roundhouse to 39 stalls, forming almost a complete circle. The new addition was of brick construction on concrete foundations, the stalls were 100 feet in length with 65-foot engine pits. The annexed machine shop, 52 by 140 feet, included a blacksmith's shop and what is described as the fan room, from whence hot air was circulated to the roundhouse by means of an underground concrete duct and to the machine shop by an overhead galvanized pipe. The roofing was the standard tar and gravel, and the roof was supported by steel trusses, a modern feature. Whether this feature extended to the older part of the roundhouse is unknown. An 85-foot turntable replaced the 75-foot one. The steel trusses and hot-blast heating are the two progressive features in the design; noteworthy too is the fact that the Joffre roundhouse is extant and still in service (see Appendix A).[61]

---

59 *American Railway Engineering Association Proceedings,* Vol. 36, 1935, pp. 105-7 *passim.*
60 Ibid., Vol. 36, 1935, p. 107.
61 *Canadian Railway and Marine World,* Jan. 1922, p. 11.

Neebing Roundhouse, Fort William, Ontario. Another extant round house (see Appendix A) is that at Neebing, on the outskirts of what today is known as Thunder Bay. Plans for this roundhouse were drawn up in July 1923, and it was probably built that year or the year following. The Neebing roundhouse was originally built with 24 stalls, to which there may have been subsequent additions, all but two of which were 100 feet in length, and two were 130 feet. The foundations were concrete, which went 5 feet below grade and rested on piles. According to *Railway and Marine World*, the walls were of brick, but a draftsman's drawing in the CNR Winnipeg office shows them as concrete blocks. The roof was described as "timber frame and mill type," supporting 5-ply tar and gravel. The engine pits were 80 feet in length, and drop pit facilities were provided in the two long stalls. Firewalls divided the roundhouse into four bays of six stalls each. Windows along the back or perimeter wall measured 14 feet in height by 6 in width. The roundhouse was served by an 85-foot twin-span turntable.[62]

There were three annexes to the roundhouse as originally built (hence the past tense, for currently there is no information on the extant structure, nor has the author seen it): a machine shop, boiler room and accommodation for the staff. The machine shop measured 50 by 80 feet, the boiler room was 40 feet square (housing two 150-horsepower locomotive-type boilers), and the crews' amenities (lunchroom, locker room and washroom) were comprised in a 48-by-95-foot annex. The air compressor was electrically driven.[63]

The aforementioned roundhouse was not the first one at what was then known as Port Arthur. There were various earlier structures, long since demolished, dating from the early days of Canadian Northern construction in that part of the province, a line which became Canada's second transcontinental railway. A machine/boiler house is believed to be the only surviving component of an earlier roundhouse.

Information supplied by J. Norman Lowe indicates a 10-stall roundhouse in 1910, built at a cost of $36,320, to which a 6-stall extension was added in 1916 at a cost of $26,792 and five more stalls for $42,961 in 1919. In 1916 a machine shop was built, whether as an annex or adjacent building has not been determined, at a cost of $13,000, and a $12,000 extension was added in 1921.

Whether this structure was demolished with the completion of the new roundhouse is not known at time of writing.

Although the design of the Neebing roundhouse made reasonable provision for fire prevention, the heating system strikes one as rather dated, particularly in view of the severity of the climate. Direct-steam heat was resorted to, with low-pressure steam coils installed in the engine pits. The Neebing roundhouse was similar in design to one in Moncton, New Brunswick, put up in 1921 and no longer in existence.[64]

The Pas, Manitoba. Built in 1927 at a cost of $120,000, The Pas roundhouse has survived to the present and at last report was still in use, although in poor condition and not suitable in its new role as a diesel maintenance shop.

Plans drawn up in 1926 called for a 5-stall engine house, with stalls a little over 105 feet in length, varying in width from 15 feet at the front to 30 feet at the back. Pits built of concrete were 83 feet in length by 4 in width. One pit was designed for the handling of driving wheels, and a second for the smaller tender wheels. The overall dimensions of the engine house were 170 by 105 by 75 feet. The boiler room annex was 52 by 93 feet, which included an air compressor room, tool room, and lavatory. Neighbouring structures included a bunkhouse and

---

62 Engineer's Office, CNR Regional Office, Winnipeg, drawing 120-174, sheet 78-1.
63 *Canadian Railway and Marine World*, July 1923, pp. 322-23.
64 Ibid.

stores building. The stall doors measured 12 feet in height. Both the foundations and the walls were built of concrete, as was the floor. The roof posts were 12-by-12-inch timbers, all of which had to be replaced in 1961, after nearly 35 years. The windows were of glass and concrete block, and the ceiling of 2 by 4 decking. A combination of steam and electric heat was used to cope with the severity of the winter in that latitude. In 1961 the coal-fired boilers were replaced by oil. From this description it is apparent that there is nothing in any way unusual about the The Pas roundhouse; rather it was typical of such structures in the steam era.[65]

CNR's Toronto Spadina Avenue Roundhouse. Within a few years a trio of roundhouses was built embodying the latest advances in facilities, if not in structural design. The first of these was the CNR's principal terminal roundhouse at Toronto, built in 1927 within a stone's throw of the Spadina Avenue overpass, from which one could overlook the smoky cauldron and ponderous activity of the city's newest railway facility.

Conventional in outward appearance with its brick walls, the CNR's Spadina engine house embodied a number of quite recently devised facilities: electromagnetic jacks, a boiler washing plant, a monorail connection from roundhouse to machine shop, and a cinder plant of special design, to name a few.

The design was drawn up by CNR structural engineers and architects, and the principal contractor was Anglin-Norcross Ltd. The McArthur Concrete Pile Company contracted for the piling on which the foundations were set, and the 160-foot brick chimney was by Francis Hankin and Company. The Spadina Avenue roundhouse (as it is referred to in these pages) was begun on 17 May 1926 and opened on 2 February 1927.[66]

The foundations are concrete, supported on concrete piles, the walls brick, and the house framing timber, presumably roof posts, beams, etc. The roof, "mill type timber frame" covered with tarred felt, pitch and gravel, is similar to that on the Neebing roundhouse and cannot be considered as other than conservative design by this date. A special feature of the roof was that on the inner part of the house it was designed with a slope in both directions for more efficient drainage. The house was built with 36 stalls, with space for nine more if needed; eight of the stalls were 130 feet in length, and the rest 110 feet. The engine pits were nearly 87 feet in length. There were three drop pits equipped with electromagnetic hoisting jacks — one to handle the driving wheels, one for locomotive truck wheels and one for tender wheels. A monorail system led from the driving wheel drop pit to the machine shop, the first instance of such a facility to our knowledge in Canada. The architect provided three interior firewalls, a safety provision. From the general description the structure can scarcely be considered fireproof, though it was no doubt fire-resistant.[67]

The Toronto Spadina engine house boasted an improved smoke removal system about which the company was enthusiastic. Instead of relying on the individual smoke jack at each stall, with its bell-shaped hood, the CNR engineers devised a timber and transite duct measuring 4 by 5½ feet, which extended all round the house and into which movable cast-iron smoke jacks discharged the emissions from the locomotives. This duct in turn was exhausted into a 160-foot chimney by a powerful fan housed in an annex known as the fan house. The system was said to result in a relatively smoke-free roundhouse. Another special feature of this roundhouse was the boiler washing plant, consisting of two large tanks into which steam and hot water from the boilers of incoming engines was discharged, processed, and hot water returned to the locomotive boilers for fill up.[68]

65   Engineer's Office CNR Regional Office, Winnipeg, plan no. 120-163, Hudson Bay Railway, July 1926;
      Ibid., file 1835-T-16.
66   *Canadian Railway and Marine World,* April 1927, p. 190; Ibid., Feb. 1933, p. 68.
67   Ibid., April 1927, pp. 186-7.
68   Ibid.

Neebing roundhouse, Thunder Bay, Ontario, 1990. — Greg McDonnell

Spadina roundhouse from CN tower, 1976. — Greg McDonnell

The heating system was indirect steam supplied by the city of Toronto Terminals Railway Company plant and fed through coils in the fan room annex. The latter housed two fans. The heating fan on the ground floor forced heated air from the steam coils through a heating duct which encircled the house underground, feeding hot air to the pits and various parts of the house. On the first floor was the exhaust fan, rated at 110,000 cubic feet per minute, connected with the transite duct in the roof. The smoke and fumes were vented up the 160-foot chimney, leaving the roundhouse relatively smoke-free. This made for much better working conditions and drastically reduced the corrosive effects of exhaust gases, which were discharged into the air high above the ground rather than a few feet above the roof line from each stall. The heating fan was used for ventilation purposes in the heat of summer.[69]

The machine shop annex, 80 by 160 feet, was also of steel-frame brick construction on concrete foundations, the same as the roundhouse proper. Timbers were used in the roof which, like the roundhouse, consisted of the more or less standard felt, tar and gravel. Three ceiling-mounted unit heaters circulated warmed air from steam coils by means of a fan, the same units used for ventilation and cool air circulation in summer. Unit heaters became widely used, almost to the exclusion of any other system in the years ahead. While it is not known whether the Toronto Spadina Avenue machine shop initiated their use by Canadian railways, it is safe to say that this at least was an early instance of unit reinforced-concrete construction, with the same type of foundation as the rest of the complex, viz., concrete on concrete piles. This, like the fan room, was a two-storey structure. The basement was utilized for oil storage tanks, the ground floor served as a storeroom, stores office, locomotive crew equipment room and lavatory. On the upper floor were to be found the general office, crew booking-in office, the foreman's office, lunchroom and storeroom. The foreman's office commanded a full view of the length of the machine shop. Finally there was an arch brick and casting stores annex, measuring 30 by 65 feet, of similar construction to the rest of the complex, featuring outsize wall windows and storage for heavy castings and firebox arch brick.[70]

Associated with the Spadina Avenue roundhouse was a cinder-handling plant, the second of its type installed in Canada, the first being at the previously described Neebing CNR roundhouse at Fort William. The ash pits located beneath the coal hoppers on five approach tracks were designed with a continuous chain conveyor, which rose on an incline, discharging into gondola cars on the cinder track. This system resembles that developed at the Chicago National Consolidated Locomotive Terminal in 1922, except that the latter was inside the roundhouse, the cinder disposal facility combined with the engine pit, whereas the CNR's Spadina Avenue facility was outside the roundhouse. Also exterior to the roundhouse at the Spadina yards was a coaling and sand plant of advanced design, a reinforced-concrete structure of 600-ton capacity. Coal was discharged into locomotive tenders from six 100-ton circular bins and sand was supplied from chutes between the coal bins, the sand being dried and hoisted to the bins by compressed air. In 1928 this was the largest locomotive coaling and sanding plant on the CNR.

The Toronto Spadina Avenue roundhouse was supplied with one of the new-style twin-span turntables, 100 feet in length, a design which did not require balancing of the load before operating, more specific details of which will appear in a later context. Further special features of the roundhouse included double-sheathed doors, the use of what was known as "leadized" pipe, resistant to acid-bearing gases, used for the first time in a Canadian round-house, and a specially designed wall allowing an out-of-control locomotive to pass through

---

69   Ibid.
70   Ibid.

with minimum damage to the wall as a whole. Finally the CNR's Spadina roundhouse was among the first to heat by indirect radiation.[71]

The Toronto Spadina Avenue roundhouse was in active use into the mid-1980s, busily serving the diesel as it had steam locomotives not so many years ago. Within a couple of years after completion, this roundhouse was to have a closely contiguous neighbour erected by the rival CPR almost within a stone's throw.

John Street CPR Roundhouse, Toronto. The original 15-stall CPR John Street roundhouse was built in 1897, with additions in 1907 and 1918. With the opening of the new 32-stall roundhouse on this site late in October 1929, the old roundhouse was at once demolished. To illustrate the increasing size of locomotives, and hence of the facilities to house and service them, the John Street stalls in 1897 were 70 feet in length, increased to 80 feet in 1907, to 85 feet in 1918, and in 1929 to 110 and to 130 feet. The main contract went to Anglin-Norcross, Toronto, the same firm which had the construction contract for CNR's Spadina roundhouse a little over two years before. The 3-point turntable was 120 feet in length, compared with the original 70-foot turntable in 1897. Like its CNR neighbour, the CPR John Street structure was built on concrete foundations, with piles sunk to bedrock, and the walls were brick, likewise the roof was mill type, with tar and gravel roofing. In all particulars, the two roundhouses resembled one another closely. The floor and engine pits were concrete throughout. The monitor roof may be clearly seen in the line drawing showing a longitudinal view of the interior, from which it will be apparent that the monitor rose a little higher on one side than the other, the ceiling on the high side being nearly 33 feet from the floor. The cement piles and foundations are clearly shown. The monitor was glazed on both sides, the windows hinged from the top. The side walls had spacious windows which together with the monitor windows gave excellent light.

The outstanding feature of this roundhouse was its direct-steaming facility, the first such in Canada, although closely followed by the TH&B's Hamilton roundhouse. As previously described, the fires were drawn at the ash pit, and once in the roundhouse, the boiler was connected to a steam line which maintained boiler pressure at a reduced level, being increased to the operating level when the locomotive was ready for the road. At the firing-up track the coal, which had been thinly spread on the grates after the fire was drawn, was ignited by a portable oil torch and rapidly readied for the road. As with the neighbouring CNR roundhouse, this one drew its steam from the Toronto Terminal Railway's central heating plant located at nearby York and Fleet streets. As with the CNR Spadina roundhouse, the John Street roundhouse was equipped with boiler blowout and washout connections. Heating was similar to the system in the CNR engine house.

Direct steaming offered several advantages, the most obvious of which was faster handling of locomotives. Moreover, with direct steaming locomotives were always dispatched with a clean fire, making for more efficient operation. Also, boilers filled with a mixture of hot water and steam, as was the practice with direct steaming, heated more uniformly, increasing operational efficiency of the locomotive. Direct steaming made for better working conditions in the roundhouse, with the elimination of smoke and gases ever present in some measure despite the use of smoke jacks. Lighting within the roundhouse was also improved with the elimination of smoke and steam, not to mention the reduction in the noise level, since boilers no longer needed to be blown into the air through use of the steam-stack blowers. Not only that, but stationary boilers, which could use low-grade coal, were more efficient than locomotive boilers, hence there was a savings in fuel in raising steam to ready the locomotive for the road. Hitherto it had been found that locomotive boilers operated at their

---

71   Ibid., Nov. 1928, pp. 633, 640-3 *passim*.

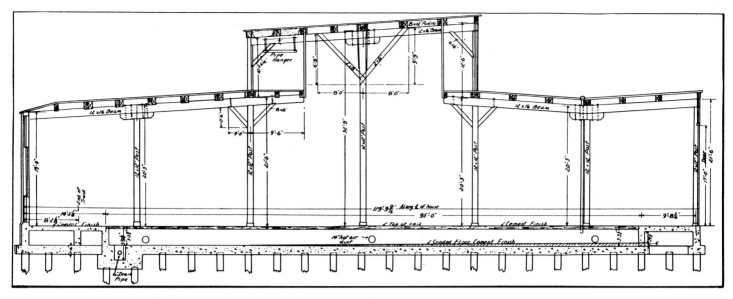

Longitudinal drawing of the Toronto CPR roundhouse. – *Canadian Railway & Marine World*, Dec. 1929

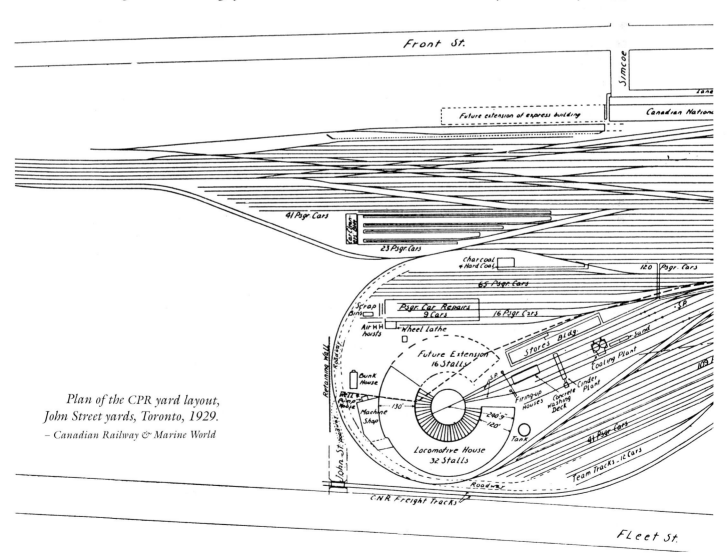

Plan of the CPR yard layout,
John Street yards, Toronto, 1929.

– *Canadian Railway & Marine World*

Interior John Street roundhouse, 1981.

– Greg McDonnell

John St., Toronto, 1983.

– Greg McDonnell

nadir of efficiency during the firing-up process, while burning relatively high-grade and expensive coal. The direct-steaming equipment was designed by the Railway Engineering Equipment Company, Chicago, and the contract for its installation was taken by the F.W. Miller Heating Company. By the time this roundhouse was opened, it is noteworthy that there were only about a half dozen such facilities in the whole of the U.S.

The CPR yard complex is clearly seen in the drawing showing the location of the 32-stall roundhouse at Fleet and John streets, with its machine shop annex on the west side of the roundhouse, and adjacent facilities – 60,000 gallon water tank, bunkhouse, stores building, coaling plant, cinder plant, and wash-out facilities. To the north and east are the multiple tracks of the passenger yards, which 50 years ago were filled with cars of all descriptions.

The machine shop, snuggled against the west wall of the roundhouse, was extensively equipped with lathes and shaper drills and included a blacksmith's shop, compressor room, locker room and lavatory within its 84-by 178-foot dimensions. The fan room also opened off the machine shop.

Both engine houses were quite modern structures by the standards of their time and survived more than two decades after the passing of the last steam locomotive.

Hamilton's TH&B Roundhouse. In the summer of 1929 the Toronto, Hamilton & Buffalo Railway let contracts for the building of a 27-stall roundhouse which when completed compared closely with the two Toronto houses already described, both as to construction and facilities provided. Twenty of the stalls were of 110-foot length and seven were 155 feet. The whole structure formed a little over a half circle. Like the CN Spadina yard and CP John Street structure, the new TH&B roundhouse in Hamilton was built on concrete foundations, on which rose brick walls. The main construction contractor was the Dominion Construction Company with W.H. Cooper, and the 100-foot, 3-point turntable was put in by Canadian Bridge Co., Walkerville, Ontario. Steel trusses of 60 and 72-foot length supported the monitor roof. The floor was concrete and the windows were wood throughout. The TH&B house employed unit hot-air heaters, like the CNR Spadina machine shop. The unit heaters supplied hot air to the roundhouse through underground ducts. The 80-by-160-foot machine shop annex was of concrete and brick construction similar to the roundhouse proper, with a steel-truss roof. The floors were concrete and asphalt. Annexed to the end of the machine shop was the blacksmith's, spring and flue shop, similar in construction to the rest of the structure, measuring 60 by 80 feet. The roundhouse had two drop pits for the removal of wheels, a telfer or monorail by overhead suspension leading from the roundhouse into the machine shop. The stores building was separately housed but adjacent to the roundhouse and was also of brick construction.

The structure was designed with a monitor roof, fitted with extensive windows. The wooden stall doors, 17 feet in height and 7 feet 6 inches in breadth, were probably pine. There are no transoms, at least at the present time, although there may have been originally. The joists, columns, girders and corbels were of Douglas fir, and the door guards and interior window casings were of pine, as were the roof boards. The roofing was the commonly used tarred felt, and the roof ventilators were copper. The firewalls were of lightweight tile. All window sills and copings were of pre-cast concrete.

Two unit heaters with turbine-driven fans served the 110-foot stall section of the roundhouse, and wall unit heaters the 155-foot stalls, capable of maintaining a temperature of 60 degrees Fahrenheit in the roundhouse proper and 65 degrees in the machine shop, with an outside temperature of zero. Cast-iron steam radiators heated the offices off the machine shop to maintain a temperature of 70 degrees.

The Hamilton TH&B roundhouse was the second in Canada to provide direct-steaming facilities, available in 20 of its 27 stalls, with blow-off, boiler refill and steam lines. Boiler pressure of 225 pounds was supplied to locomotives readied for the road. The powerhouse

TH&B, Hamilton, Ontario, from coal tower, 1985. — Greg McDonnell

was a 65-by-130-foot brick-and-concrete structure adjacent to the roundhouse, from which rose a 175-foot chimney of 8 foot inside diameter. The roof was steel trussed and windows steel sashed. Three 260-horsepower boilers supplied the steam for heat, the air compressor, the boiler washing and filling pumps. On leaving the roundhouse, locomotives were fired up to operating pressure in as little as two minutes. The company claimed for direct steaming, besides speedy dispatching, savings in fuel, reduced boiler maintenance, reduced labour costs in the roundhouse, smoke abatement, better working conditions and, perhaps not least, reduced fire hazard.

Moving outside the roundhouse there was a reinforced-concrete coaling plant of 300 tons capacity. The automatic plant was electrically powered and could handle 75 tons per hour. Unlike the two Toronto roundhouses, which relied on the city for steam, the Hamilton house raised its own, in the manner of all engine houses providing more than rudimentary shelter and turnaround facilities. The adjacent sand house, 20 by 80 feet, utilized a steam sand dryer and sand-elevating drum driven by compressed air, from whence the sand was conveyed to bins in the coaling plant structure, and from there by overhead spouts to the sand domes of locomotives as required. A cinder-handling plant, electrically operated, removed cinders and ash by means of buckets of 80-cubic-foot capacity. As with the new CNR and CPR roundhouses in Toronto, the cinder plant was still an outdoor facility separate from the roundhouse, although perhaps similar in operation to that at Chicago's National Consolidated Locomotive Terminal developed in 1923.

The Hamilton roundhouse was well equipped. There were three electrically operated drop tables of 50 tons capacity each at the three drop pits; the drop table for the driver wheels was 8 feet in length by 10 feet 6 inches in breadth, while the two for the pony, trailer and tender wheels were 5 feet 6 inches in length by the same width, all three clearing the pit walls by 2 inches. The track tables were operated by means of a four-screw electrically powered gearing device capable of operating the table, with a load of up to 50 tons, at a speed of 12 inches per minute. The screws were made of forged steel and they were mounted on a 4-wheel travelling carriage of structural steel. The traverse gearing, on the other hand, was manual. The motor operating each jack was a Westinghouse 220-volt AC. The drop pits were also served by a 10-ton electric hoist, with electric trolley, running on an overhead 24-inch I-beam, the hoist also electrically operated. By means of this equipment heavy parts could more easily be moved safely to the machine shop.

Adjoining the machine shop was the facilities building, long and narrow (18½ by 103 feet), a two-storey concrete-and-brick structure housing the foreman's office, dispatcher's office, registering or crew room, locker room, lavatory and a first-aid room on the ground floor. On the second floor were found a supply room, washroom, and shopmen's and locomotive crews' room. A separate office building, of two-storey brick-and-concrete construction with hardwood floors completed the complex. Such was the Hamilton TH&B roundhouse, which with the aforementioned CNR and CPR Toronto roundhouses probably provided the most advanced facilities available in Canadian terminal yards in 1930. At that time there must have been few who foresaw the attenuated afterlife to which the roundhouse was to be condemned within another 30 years by the demise of the locomotive for which they were designed. The TH&B Hamilton roundhouse is among the few which have survived to serve the diesels.[72]

Sundry Roundhouses to the End of the Steam Era. A September 1932 issue of *Canadian Railway and Marine World* described in detail the introduction in the summer of 1931 of portable oil torches for firing up locomotives quickly at the CNR's Toronto Danforth

---

72 *Canadian Railway and Marine World*, Feb. 1930, pp. 82.

roundhouse. It would appear, however, that this technique had been introduced two years previously at the CPR's John Street roundhouse in Toronto. On the other hand, the Danforth roundhouse technique may have broken new ground in Canadian yards because the latter equipment was described as a portable oil burner, made up of pipe and fittings in the form of a flexible lead, which inserted through the firebox door before any coal was laid on the grates. The burner raised steam pressure to 140 to 150 pounds in about an hour and a half. Once this pressure was reached, the burner was removed and the grates stoked with coal. The system was economical providing the cost of oil did not exceed $2^1/_2$ times that of coal. The oil emitted from the burner was atomized by compressed air. The system had been devised at the instigation of the city to reduce air pollution.[73]

The CPR John Street apparatus was used to fire up coal after boiler pressure had been raised in the roundhouse by the direct-steaming technique, whereas the CNR Danforth equipment was used in lieu of a coal fire in the firebox to raise steam from the start to a certain level before stoking the firebox. Nonetheless it appears that the equipment was of similar design and, if so, the CPR preceded the CNR in this technique by about two years.

In 1937 the T&NO built a new 6-stall roundhouse at Timmins to replace one originally built in South Porcupine and subsequently dismantled and moved to Timmins in 1926. The whole complex, including turntable and cinder hoist, was put up by company labour for $71,295.85. The structure, set on concrete foundations, from the brief description on company plans and local information, was apparently frame throughout, with framework of British Columbia fir and exterior walls of cove siding. The stalls, just short of 100 feet in length, had cinder floors. Within the roundhouse were housed the car foreman's office, the electrical shop, storeroom, machine shop, locomotive foreman's office and washroom, all with 3-inch plank floors. Annexed at the back of the structure was the boiler room and coal shed; the boilers are now oil-fired. The Timmins roundhouse's spacious windows and freshly painted sash and siding is shown in recent photographs. The 90-foot air-operated turntable was built by the Canadian Bridge Company, Walkerville, Ontario, in 1936 at a cost installed of $19,257. The transition from steam to diesel power called for the installation of a forced-air ventilating system, since the smoke jacks did not carry off the diesel fumes adequately. In 1956 or 1957 the original timber floor was replaced with concrete, and in 1966 the coal-fired boilers gave way to automatic oil-fired, at a great savings in labour. Further modifications in the late 1960s included provision of a lunchroom within the roundhouse and the conversion of one stall, from which the rails were removed, to a bus garage.[74]

It may well be asked what is significant about the Timmins roundhouse. Perhaps only that a terminal roundhouse should have been built of wood as late as 1937, and that on one of the country's more progressive railways, as witness its early conversion to diesel power. The Timmins roundhouse is another survivor from the steam era, serving adequately a function for which it was not designed.

A post-war construction at Arvida Quebec, on the Roberval & Saguenay Railway, is of possible interest by reason of its comparatively recent date. The actual construction date is unknown, but the company draftsman's drawings are dated 28 August 1944 and 7 June 1945. Set on concrete foundations extending 4 feet above grade, the 9-stall Arvida roundhouse was of brick construction, with a 4-ply felt-and-gravel roofing laid on gypsum slabs, which would render the structure largely fireproof. The foundations were 13 inches thick and the walls

73 Ibid., Sept. 1932, pp. 445-7 *passim*.
74 Engineer's Office, ONR North Bay, file 1835-37, section 4; draftsman's drawings Timmins roundhouse; file 1835-37, "old section no. 1"; file 1835-37, section 4; letter Brian Craig, ONR office North Bay, 11 June 1981.

*Timmins, Ontario, roundhouse
showing wood construction, ONR 1982.*

– photo by author

St. Thomas, Ontario, 1982.

– Greg McDonnell

Aerial view of the CPR St. Luc roundhouse, Montreal, 1950.   – CP Archives

12$\frac{1}{2}$ inches, no doubt because of the severity of the climate. The 13-by-11-foot windows each had 15 panes of glass or lights. The Arvida roundhouse is still in use.[75]

Another roundhouse of comparatively recent date, built at St. Thomas, Ontario, in 1941 by an American road, the Père Marquette, cutting across the Ontario peninsula from Detroit to Buffalo, merits passing notice, if only for purposes of comparison with more or less contemporary Canadian structures. The 8-stall St. Thomas roundhouse, also still in service with wood frame and brick walls, had a monitor roof rising 30 feet above the floor at its highest point. The stalls were 120 feet and the turntable was 115 feet indicative of the size of locomotives in service on the road, taken over by the Chesapeake & Ohio in 1947. From the brief description this roundhouse resembles Canadian contemporaries.[76]

The last roundhouse to be built in Canada, and possibly in North America, is the CPR St. Luc roundhouse at Montreal. Entirely fireproof, with frame of reinforced concrete and brick walls, this 36-stall roundhouse embodied many of the latest ideas on roundhouse design when opened in 1949. Twenty-seven of the stalls are 130 feet in length and ten 140 feet. As may readily be seen, the St. Luc roundhouse, planned in conjunction with the new hump yard, presents a very clean appearance. From above, the monitor roof gives the appearance of concentric rings and is unbroken by smoke jacks, for it goes without saying that by this date the St. Luc facility utilized direct steaming, introduced more than 20 years previously. The turntable was a 110-foot twin-span type. At the time of writing there are no further details on construction. In 1950 the roundhouse housed both steam and diesel-electric locomotives, for at this time the Canadian roads were in the midst of diesel conversion. The CPR St. Luc roundhouse is still in railroad use, although not as a roundhouse per se. Part of it is now used to house diesels pending dispatch to neighbouring repair shops and part for sundry other purposes such as storage. The St. Luc roundhouse, embodying the latest features and design, was fated to pass quickly into obsolescence soon after it was built.[77]

The predominance of the roundhouse should not lead to the assumption that it was the sole form of engine house, even in Canada. The following chapter will deal with its alternative, Berg's "square house."

---

75 Roberval and Saugenay Railway Co., drawings.
76 Chesapeake and Ohio Historical Society, Alderson, West Virgina, draftsman's drawing.
77 CPR Archives, photo no. 11991 and 14884; Omer Lavallée, CPR archivist and historian; *Canadian Transportation,* July 1950, p. 367.

Engine Houses and Engine Sheds

In this chapter, two themes will be discussed: the large rectangular engine houses which were built at Sault Ste. Marie and at Hornepayne, Ontario, unique in Canada and unusual on this continent; and the small rectangular house best described as an engine shed. In dealing with the Sault Ste. Marie and Hornepayne structures first, it is not suggested that these are necessarily more significant in the historical context; indeed the contrary may be the case if representativeness is considered an important criterion in determining historical importance.

THE BIG HOUSE: TWO OF A KIND

In seeking precedents for the two remarkable structures at Sault Ste. Marie and at Hornepayne, built in 1912 and 1921 respectively, one turns to the history of American and British railroading. Given the intertwined and almost inextricable connection between American and Canadian railroad enterprise, logically one would look to the United States for the origins of this design, notwithstanding the decided American preference for the roundhouse for all but small structures housing less than a dozen to about 20 locomotives. It may well be that further research will uncover an American origin, but at the present stage of study, all that can be said is that the Sault Ste. Marie structure was built by a Chicago firm to the design of an American architect. For precedents we are thrown back to England, home of the steam locomotive.

The earliest engine house on which the Sault Ste. Marie and the Hornepayne engine houses may have been pattered in terms of layout and overall design was a much larger one built as early as 1859 for the North-Eastern Railway at Newcastle-on-Tyne. This structure, surely massive by the standards of the time, measured 450 feet in length by 280 in breadth, housing no fewer than five 42-foot interconnecting turntables. It was calculated that this engine house at Newcastle had the overall accommodation of five roundhouses at the time, with a 37 percent reduction in wall footage. There were five roof spans running the length of the building, the three central ones of 65 feet and the two outer ones of 42 feet 6 inches, all of which were supported by cast-iron columns or posts at 25-foot intervals. The company claimed that the construction costs of the Newcastle engine house were much lower than for a roundhouse of equivalent size. Further examples of this type of British engine house with interior turntables may be cited. In 1907 the Great Western Railway opened a 360-by-444 foot engine house at Old Oak Common, three miles west of the Paddington London terminal, with accommodation for 112 locomotives in stalls varying in length from 41 to 82 feet. (English locomotives by this date were much smaller than Canadian locomotives.) The Old Oak Common engine house had four interior 65-foot electrically operated turntables, each of which served 28 radial tracks, a layout similar to the Canadian engine houses at Sault Ste. Marie and Hornepayne except that the latter had a single turntable each rather than four. Annexes along the sides of the structure housed a repair shop, stores, blacksmith's, coppersmith's and carpenter's shop, kitchen, two mess rooms, and a sand and furnace room. Construction was of brick on concrete foundations, roof posts were of cast-iron or steel, girders were of steel. The designer of the Old Oak Common engine house was G.J. Churchyard, described simply as a locomotive engineer with the GWR. He advocated this design for engine houses accommodating 100 locomotives or more, and the engine house with longitudinal track layout for smaller houses. Churchyard designed a similar structure at Swindon on the GWR, illustrated by the line drawing. The Swindon engine house was of similar dimensions to Old Oak Common, with four interior 65-foot turntables, each with 28 radiating stub tracks. Annexed along the sides were two sand furnace rooms, two mess rooms with intervening kitchen, locker room, blacksmith's, coppersmith's and carpenter's shop at one

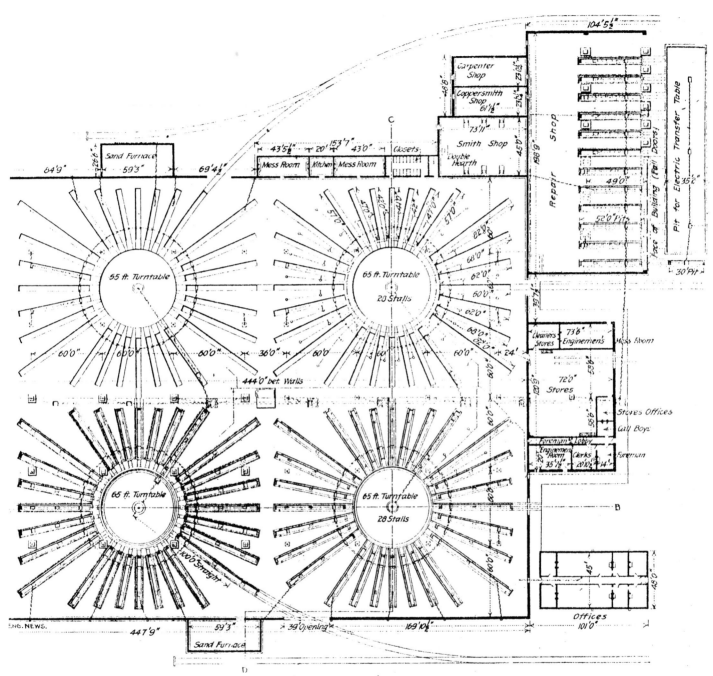

FIG. 1. PLAN OF RECTANGULAR ENGINE HOUSE WITH GROUPS OF RADIAL TRACKS AT SWINDON, ENGLAND; GREAT WESTERN F
G. J. Churchward, Locomotive Engineer.

Plan drawing of the rectangular engine house, Swindon, England, c.1907.

– NRC, *Engineering News* 1907

corner, adjoining which was a 199-by-104 foot repair shop served by a transfer table, and a stores building. Only the general concept is common to this structure and the two Canadian houses, and these two engine houses designed by Churchyard and built sometime about 1907 are described in some detail because, for want of further evidence, they appear to be the progenitors of the Sault Ste. Marie and Hornepayne engine houses.[1]

On the surmise that the inspiration for the unusual design of the Sault Ste. Marie engine house was actually American, one could cite a description in an October 1912 issue of *Engineering News* concerning an engine house under construction on the Missouri, Oklahoma & Gulf Railroad at Muskogee, Oklahoma. The Muskogee engine house was built by W.H. Rosecrans Engineering Company, a Chicago firm, as was the builder of the Sault Ste. Marie engine house, the Arnold Company. Also of interest is the reference in *Engineering News* to other engine houses of this design unusual in the U.S. The Muskogee house was initially 94 by 110 feet, with provision to lengthen it to 220 feet, within which were four tracks. Unlike the two Canadian houses, this one was of the "run-through" type, with exits at both ends. The editor of *Engineering News* compared the much cheaper construction of this type of engine house to that of an equivalent roundhouse, and indeed contended that the rectangular house merited more serious consideration by American railroaders.[2]

Algoma Central's Sault Ste. Marie Engine House

Designed by P.L. Battey, chief engineer of the Arnold Company of Chicago, and built under contract by this firm for the Algoma Central & Hudson Bay Railway at its Sault Ste. Marie, Ontario, terminal in 1912, this engine house was unique in Canada until 1921, when one of similar design was built by the Canadian National Railways 190 miles to the north, at Hornepayne. To the author's knowledge no others of similar design were built anywhere in Canada. It bears repeating that these two engine houses are not to be confused with the stub-track or run-through type of rectangular house or shed, to be dealt with later in this chapter, for the Sault Ste. Marie and Hornepayne houses had interior turntables and were on an altogether different scale.[3]

The Arnold Company contracted for construction of the engine house, the annexed machine shop, store building, coaling station and ash pit, besides the installation of all the machinery, at a final overall cost of $351,841.49, exceeding the estimate by 15.5 percent, by reason of increased costs for excavation, brickwork and labour, among other things. The outer dimensions are 266 by 179 feet, and the roof trusses clear the roof by 18 feet at all points. The foundations are concrete up to the window sills, and the walls are 13-inch-thick brick. Six monitor roofs run the length of the engine house, fitted with 4-foot continuous steel sash and windows, an exterior view at one corner of which is shown in a recent photograph. The glass brick windows are a recent installation, for originally these were of glass. The monitor windows are still glazed, but those in the walls have been fitted with a translucent brick, as noted. Roof trusses of structural steel support the roof, each of the sides spans 44 feet in length, and the centre span above the turntable is 88 feet, supporting two monitors, whereas the other five supported one. The engine house completely enclosed an 80-foot deck turntable from which radiated 14 locomotive pit tracks, two of which had driving-wheel drop pits, and two had truck-and-tender wheel drop pits.[4]

---

1   Marcus Binney and David Pearce, op. cit., pp. 165, 167, 171; *The Civil Engineer and Architects Journal*, 1 May 1859, p. 132; *Engineering News*, 13 June 1907, pp. 642-3.
2   Ibid., 24 Oct. 1912, pp. 776-7.
3   *Canadian Railway and Marine World*, Jan. 1922, p. 13.
4   Engineer's Office, Algoma Central Railway, Sault Ste. Marie, company records — letter Arnold Co., 30 April 1913, statement of costs ACR shops, draftsman's profile 5 April 1912.

Corner view of the ACR engine house, Sault Ste. Marie, Ontario.

– photo by author, 1982

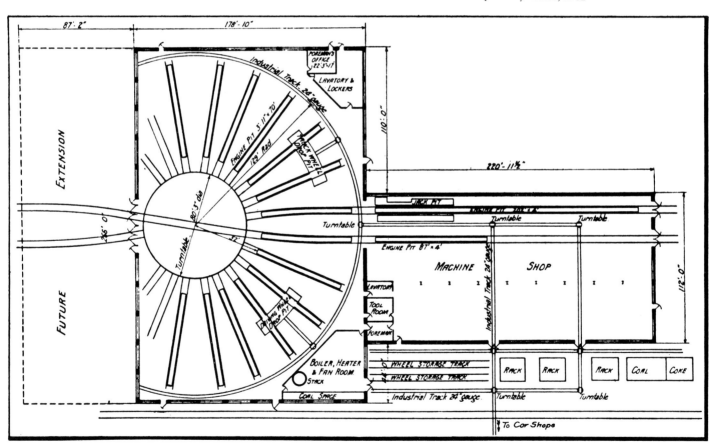

Draftsman's plan of the ACR engine house, Sault Ste. Marie, 1913.   – NAC, National Library

Natural light within the engine house is good, for each monitor was hung with continuous steel sash hinging at the top, controlled from the floor by worm and gear gangs; the monitor windows were so designed as to exclude rain even when fully open. The monitors drained onto the lower main roof, which is saddled to drain water to wrought-iron downspouts.[5]

The walls were concrete to a point $5\frac{1}{2}$ feet above grade; the brick walls were built with pilasters 3 feet wide and 17 inches thick, and spaced at 22 foot intervals. The wall windows, 19 feet in width by 14 in height, were set in steel sash between the pilasters and anchored in brick. Above the windows projected a 4-course brick corbel.[6]

All track doors were of $\frac{3}{4}$-inch-thick wood, with glazing consisting of 15 lights; these too have been replaced with translucent but opaque glass brick. The original doors have also been replaced by the roll-top type. The original 3-ply wooden doors were fitted with wrought-iron stiffeners and heavy hinges, also a locking device of special design.[7]

The floor of the engine house was vitrified brick (glazed or hard-burnt) laid in sand on a cement base.[8]

All roof columns and roof trusses were steel. The roof itself was 2-inch wood sheath with 5-ply composition roofing. There were 14 asbestos smoke jacks. The original track in both engine house and machine shop was 80-pound rail.[9]

The reader is referred to the plan drawing for the overall layout of engine house and machine shop, from which will readily be seen that the latter, 221 feet in length and 112 in breadth, projects from the back of the engine house. A perimeter industrial track and three small turntables provide access from the drop-pit stalls of the engine house to the machine shop, standard in nearly all roundhouses. The machine shop was of similar construction in all particulars to the engine house, with which it formed an integral unit. The foreman's office, locker room and lavatory are located in the opposite corner of the engine house.[10]

The machine shop comprised two bays, one of which was 44 feet wide and the other 66 feet. A single-pitch steel truss supported the roof, with a clearance to the floor of 18 feet 2 inches, in the smaller of the two bays, and in the 66-foot-wide bay the steel roof truss cleared the floor by a full 32 feet. The roof was of different material, described as reinforced-cement tile $1\frac{3}{4}$ inches thick, laid in slabs $5\frac{1}{2}$ by 2 feet, in turn covered by 5-ply Barrett roofing (apparently a trade name of the time). The floor consisted of creosoted maple paving blocks laid in sand on a 5-inch concrete sub-base, whereas the engine house floor was laid in vitrified brick with the same sub-base of sand and cement.[11]

Sault Ste. Marie being the main terminal of the Algoma Central & Hudson Bay Railway, it follows that the machine shop was equipped for full shop work, as evidenced by the two erecting pits located on the two tracks leading in from the engine house, where locomotives could be taken down completely and reassembled. A 24-inch industrial track with turntable gave access to the machine shop bays, laid out at right angles to the erecting pits. Further to this was a 10-ton travelling crane on a girder $24\frac{1}{2}$ feet above the floor. One of the erecting pits was equipped with an electric screw jack hoist for removing the wheels from locomotives. The travelling crane rode on a runway 220 feet in length and more than 26 feet above the floor, powered by a 220-volt A.C. motor. The crane was operated from a platform offset so

5   *Canadian Railway and Marine World*, Feb. 1913, pp. 51-3.
6   Ibid.
7   Ibid.
8   Ibid.
9   Engineer's Office, ACR Sault Ste. Marie, records-estimate costs by Arnold Co., 25 May 1912.
10 Ibid.
11 *Canadian Railway and Marine World*, Feb. 1913, p. 54.

that the operator had an unimpeded view of his work at all times. The hooks were of wrought steel and the cables were of 6-stranded steel. The wheels were double-flanged.[12]

Some idea of the scope of the work carried out in the machine shop may be had from a listing of the tools and equipment therein. For example, there were in the inventory, seven different types of lathe, five drills, two forges, two furnaces, and a 400-ton hydraulic wheel press. The whole complex was heated by hot air, on the widely adopted system of indirect steam, air being circulated by a steam-driven fan through horizontal steam-heated coils, thence through underground concrete conduits for distribution to the engine pits and turntable pits by means of vitrified tile ducts, the steam supplied from the three 150-horse-power boilers at 100 pounds pressure.[13]

Algoma Central's Sault Ste. Marie engine house is in full use today, 70 years later, the only obvious changes being the substitution of translucent glass brick for the original window glazing in all the windows except the monitors, and the six metal stacks in place of the 125-foot reinforced-concrete chimney. The machinery, originally belt steam driven, has long since been converted to electricity. The turntable tractor motor was originally air driven, and presumably still is, as are a good many surviving turntable motors. All in all, the Sault Ste. Marie engine house and machine shop is a remarkable structure in Canadian railway yard industrial architecture.

Canadian National's Hornepayne Engine House

For nearly a decade the Sault engine house remained unique in Canada until in 1921 the Canadian National Railway built one of similar design nearly 200 miles due north of Sault Ste. Marie at Hornepayne, divisional point north of Lake Superior. The new engine house, especially designed for the rigorous climate of that region, replaced a 14-stall frame round-house of standard CNoR design.[14]

The 288-by-223 foot brick-and-concrete structure was designed by architect G.C. Briggs. R.S. McCormick, general superintendent and chief engineer of the Algoma Central, asserted in 1921 that the new Hornepayne structure was very similar to the ACR's at Sault Ste. Marie. In terms of structure and overall concept, this may be true, but one obvious difference is that the Hornepayne engine house is a straight rectangular structure, 223 feet 3 inches in one direction and 287 feet 7½ inches in the other, whereas the Sault Ste. Marie structure is of irregular configuration, with the rectangular machine shop projecting from the back of the engine house. The second obvious difference is one of function: the Sault Ste. Marie machine shop is nearly half the area of the engine house, whereas in Hornepayne the machine shop occupies but one corner of the engine house, indicative that the maintenance work here was less extensive than in Sault Ste. Marie. In overall dimensions the Algoma Central's Sault Ste. Marie house is bigger than the CNR's Hornepayne structure (72,000 to 64,224 square feet approximately).[15]

An idea of the building's appearance may be had from the line drawing, in front elevation, from which it is readily seen that the Hornepayne engine house had three monitors only, compared with six in the Sault Ste. Marie engine house, not to mention two more comprising the roof of the machine shop. The Hornepayne engine house gives the impression of

---

12 Ibid., Engineer's Office, ACR Sault Ste. Marie, records-estimates costs Arnold Co., 25 Nov. 1912; Ibid., specifications for electric travelling crane, Arnold Co., Chicago.

13 Ibid., specifications for machine tools, Arnold Co., *Canadian Railway and Marine World*, Feb. 1913, p. 53.

14 Canadian Northern Railway Co., *Encyclopaedia* CNR, (Montreal, 1918), p. 9; *Canadian Railway and Marine World*, Aug. 1921, p. 412-3.

15 Ibid., Jan. 1922, p. 13.

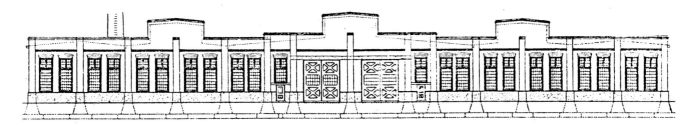

Drawing of the front elevation of the Hornepayne engine house, 1921. – NRC, *Railway Age,* Nov. 1921

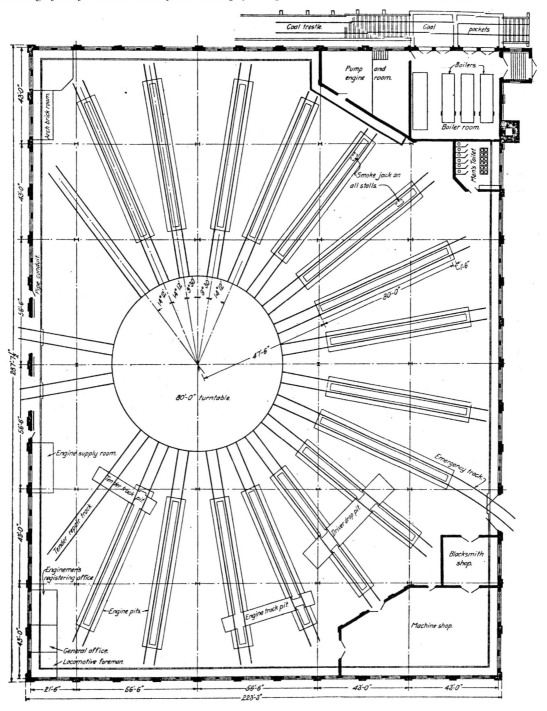

Line drawing of the floor plan for the engine house at Hornepayne, Ontario, 1921.
– NRC, *Railway Age,* Nov. 1921

Interior of the Hornepayne engine house, turntable in foreground, n.d.   – CNR

unobtrusive solidity. The interior harbours an 80-foot turntable, radiating from which are sixteen 8-foot engine pits, with two entry tracks, and one emergency exit.

The concrete foundations go 7 feet below grade to cope with the severe cold. The concrete was carried up to the level of the window sills. The rest of the wall is brick pier construction, similar to that at Sault Ste. Marie, with pilasters at 18 and 21-foot intervals. Nineteen steel columns support the steel trusses and purlins. The three monitors, fitted with steel-sashed windows on each side, run the length of the house. *Railway Age* described the roofing as "2¾-inch splined," on which was laid the usual tar, felt and gravel. The steel columns supporting the roof trusses rest on concrete pedestals whose foundations, like those of the walls, extend 7 feet below grade. A pair of double doors give access to the locomotive house at the front, on either side of which pairs of high windows are set in the front wall between the pilasters. The side walls have 11 pairs of windows interspersed in like manner. Apparently direct-steam heat was installed at the time of construction, with steam coils mounted on the walls in the engine pits.[16]

The boiler room, housing three locomotive-type boilers and measuring 43 by 40 feet, occupies one corner of the engine house, coal for the boilers (no doubt long since converted to oil-fired) being fed to the boiler room from a concrete hopper supplied by a hopper track and trestle. The pump and engine room, housing the water pumps, air compressors and electric generators, is on the other side of the boiler room, and on the other is a lavatory. In the other corner, at the rear of the engine house, is located the 40-by-74-foot machine shop and next to it, the blacksmith's shop. The general office and foreman's office occupy one of the front corners of the building, along with the enginemen's signing in and out room. At the opposite side, at the front of the building, in the days of steam, there was the brick arch room where were stored the bricks for this indispensable adjunct to the locomotive's firebox, vital to good combustion.[17]

The Hornepayne engine house, now almost 70 years old, is still in service, 25 years after the retirement of the last steam locomotive on the CNR system and 30 years since steam power disappeared from the CNR's transcontinental line.

Both the Hornepayne and the Sault Ste. Marie engine houses, built within ten years of one another in the same general region, were designed for cold winters. Sault Ste. Marie has a cold winter, and Hornepayne a colder one, but there are scores of localities north of the Great Lakes and east of the Great Divide with a comparable climate. It was claimed by proponents of the "square house" that these were easier to heat, and yet across Canada and the high plains of the trans-Mississippi West one sees roundhouses at every terminal and division point. Construction costs for houses of equivalent size were claimed to be lower for the square house. These arguments notwithstanding, Canadian and American railroads stuck with the roundhouse, although often operating in regions where one had thought that the square house with the interior turntable would have had much to recommend it. The question must for the nonce remain open.

In any case the design can scarcely be considered indigenous, since the designer of the Sault Ste. Marie house was an American and it was put up by a Chicago firm, and the construction, if not the layout, of the Hornepayne engine house was similar to that of the Soo. For all that, the two engine houses were an interesting development in the Canadian railway yard scene, if perhaps just an impressive flash in the pan.

---

16 *Railway Age,* 26 Nov. 1921, p. 1049, *Railway Mechanical Engineer,* March 1922, pp. 163-4.
17 Ibid., *Railway Age,* 26 Nov. 1921, pp. 1049 and 1051.

THE ENGINE SHED 1880S TO 1940S

In this section the illustrations unfortunately do not always correspond with the documentary information available at time of writing, but the photographs will nonetheless give the reader a good notion of these structures even when no information is available.

Engine sheds are distinguished from the small 2- to 3-stall segmented or fan-shaped "roundhouses" by reason of their parallel tracks, rather than converging tracks centred on a turntable. Since most engine sheds were small in this country, from a distance they might be mistaken for 2- or 3-stall segmented houses, but there is ever this basic distinction readily apparent on closer inspection.

An earlier chapter described a few of the rectangular and cruciform engine houses of the 1850s, chiefly on the Grand Trunk. The massive rectangular houses seen in Britain, such as the one opened in Crewe on the London & North-Western Railway in 1897 to accommodate 60 locomotives, or the London & South-Western's Eastleigh engine house, opened in 1910, 350 feet long with 15 tracks, never evolved in Canada. Nevertheless, a number of small engine sheds, with anywhere from one to four tracks, were to be found across the country, generally on branch lines, although the fan-shaped engine house was much more common.[18] The author may add that in his rambles locally on this project, he has yet to see an engine shed.

A frame engine shed was built in mid-summer 1885 at County Line Station, Cape Traverse Branch, Prince Edward Island Railway (which had in fact become a part of the government-owned ICR in 1873). This shed, with one track, was 65 feet in length, 16 in breadth and 14 in height to the eaves. As will be seen from the line drawings, the engine shed had a pitched roof. The shed was of wood construction throughout, even to the foundations, with hemlock sills 12 inches below grade. The rest of the construction was spruce — black spruce framing, the 14-foot-1-inch walls of spruce boards 9 to 11 inches in width and 1 inch thick. The slope height of the pitched roof was 8 feet 7 inches. There were six small windows, three to a side, as seen on the drawing. Curiously, no smoke jack is shown on the plan. Nor is it shown whether the County Line engine house was of the stub-track or run-through type. It is unlikely that it could have accommodated more than one locomotive, even at that early date.[19]

Ten years later, 22 June 1895, Rhodes, Curry and Company contracted for an engine shed for the ICR at Dartmouth, Nova Scotia. Apart from the 33½-foot engine pits, the Dartmouth engine shed seems to have been of entirely wood construction. Actually Rhodes and Curry contracted for two engine houses, the second located at Windsor Junction, outside Halifax. Sixty feet in length, the engine sheds were set on cedar mud sills. With a width of only 19½ feet, there would be but one track. The sheds were of the stub-track type, with one entrance, on which were hung a pair of doors 16½ feet in height and 12½ feet in breadth. The frame was built of spruce, the timbers covered with spruce boards, and the interior lined with 1-inch spruce boards. The roofing was of pine or spruce shingles. The 33½-foot engine pit was lined with stone. There was one smoke jack. Needless to add that these two structures disappeared from the scene many years ago, at an unknown date. Their significance lies in the fact that they were built at this time and place to serve a minimal requirement.[20]

A closely similar structure, in terms of size and construction, was contracted for by B.N. Mattison for the ICR at Spring Hill Junction, Nova Scotia, with the deadline of 15 September 1897. The specifications called for a rectangular structure, 70 feet in length by 19½ in width,

---

18 *Railway Age Gazette*, (New York, Simmonds-Boardman), 4 Nov. 1910, p. 841; *The Canadian Engineer*, (Toronto, Monetary Times), June 1897, p. 34.
19 PAC, RG30M; National Map Coll., deposit 22, item 445.
20 PAC, RG43C, Railways and Canals records, Vol. 33, No. 12106.

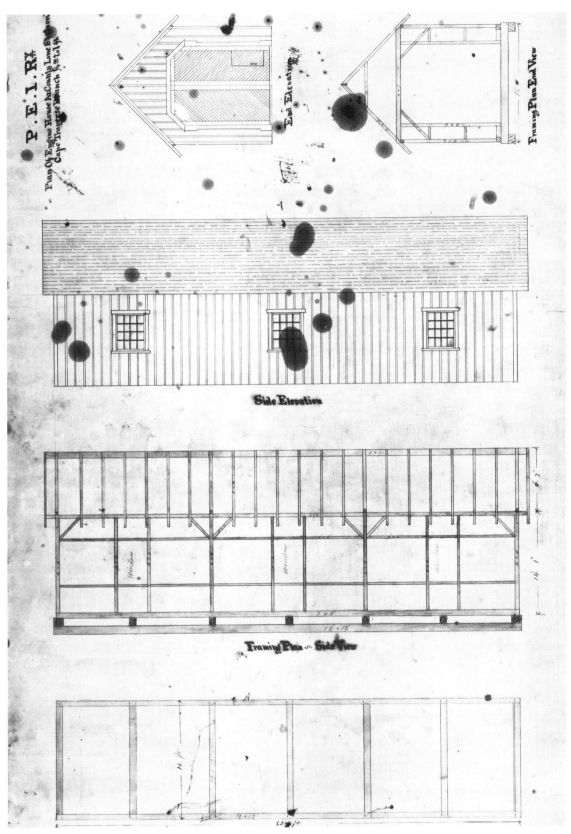

Line drawings of the PEIR engine house, County Line, Cape Traverse Branch, n.d.

– NAC, National Map Collection

Single engine shed and turntable,
Madoc, Ontario, 1929.
– CNR Archives

CPR 3-stall engine shed, Brockville, Ontario, c.1916.

– CP Archives

of spruce or pine construction. The walls on the outside were to be built of spruce or pine boards, between 8 and 11 inches in width, and the interior lined with 1-inch spruce or pine. The roof was to be of the same material. This shed too was of the stub-track type, with entrance door at one end. There were three windows on each side, each with 16 lights of 10 inch by 12 inch glazing, and there were louvred ventilators at each end of the building, in lieu of a smoke jack. The engine pit, 33½ feet in length by 4 in breadth and 2½ feet deep, was lined with stone masonry 1½ inches thick. Obviously these three ICR engine sheds, at Dartmouth, Windsor Junction and at Spring Hill Junction, were all of a pattern.[21]

The only other reference I have found to engine sheds in the Maritimes concerns two built in 1909 on the Salisbury & Harvey Railway, one at Hillsboro and the other at Albert, New Brunswick. One hundred feet in length by 30 in width, these engine sheds were designed to accommodate two locomotives and included shop facilities for minor repairs.[22]

The stark and wintry photograph, taken in 1929, is of a single-track run-through engine shed at Madoc, Ontario, on the CPR Toronto-Perth line. Photographic detail is lacking, but it appears that the structure was of wood and fitted with rectangular doors. The photograph may have been taken shortly after the shed was put up, but the shed is probably older than that. Service on this line, as far as Perth, opened in August 1884, hence there is the possibility that the engine shed may be that old.

Another photo shows in good detail a CPR engine shed at Brockville, Ontario, about 1916. There is no information on this structure at time of writing, but it may be seen from the photograph that it is 3-stalled and of frame construction. The glazing in the doors and their shape at the top, with the transom lights, was typical of early CPR engine houses. This photograph cannot be identified with information on an early Brockville CPR engine house supplied by J. Norman Lowe because Lowe describes his engine house as of stone construction, whereas judging from this photograph the construction was frame. However, it has three tracks, in accordance with Lowe's description. An intriguing point about this photograph is that from the angle at which it was taken one cannot be sure whether it was in fact a rectangular engine shed with parallel tracks or a 3-stall segmental roundhouse, a much more common structure. The caption reads "engine shed," and the author has taken it as such, but the front line of the roof may be slightly concave rather than straight, in which case its treatment does not belong in this context but an earlier one. In the absence of any documentation, the date of this engine shed can only be surmised. The CPR acquired the Brockville & Ottawa Railway in 1881, shortly after the CPR syndicate was formed, and thereafter operated the line. Presumably this engine shed was built by the CPR (on the basis of the doors and transoms), possibly in the 1880s.

Another CPR photograph, of the engine shed at Castlegar, British Columbia, taken in March 1916, is unmistakably a rectangular engine shed, of the stub-rail type judging from the background. The shed was of frame construction, with the stall doors peaked in the manner characteristic of CPR engine houses, but this one has no transom lights. This engine shed has a peaked roof, which was often the case with small rectangular engine sheds.

A photograph dated circa 1915, shows an attractive 2-stall engine shed in Maniwaki, Quebec. The shed is no longer in existence. In the absence of any documentary record it is impossible to date this engine shed. The design of the top of the doors suggests CPR styling. The Ottawa & Gatineau Valley Railway, terminating at Maniwaki, taken over by the Ottawa Northern & Western in 1902, was leased to the CPR that year, and operated by them henceforth. On the assumption that the engine shed was indeed built by the CPR, it cannot

21 Ibid., Vol. 34, No. 12843.
22 Canada. Parliament. *Sessional Papers* 1909, No. 67.

CPR 2-stall engine shed, Castlegar, British Columbia, 1916. — CP Archives

CPR 2-stall engine shed, Maniwaki, Quebec, c.1915 — CP Archives

Two-stall wooden engine house at St. Marys, Ontario. — CP Archives

Wooden engine house on the CPR at Midway, British Columbia, March 11, 1916. — CP Archives

be dated earlier than 1902 and may well have been built in 1915, when the photograph was taken, for the structure looks new. The construction is obviously frame. The roof is very slightly peaked.[23]

The Canadian Northern Railway erected a number of 2- to 4-stall frame engine sheds at sundry points, which appear in its listing published in 1918. These include a 4-stall wood-frame structure at Hudson Bay Junction, Manitoba, another of the same description at Emerson, Manitoba, and a 2-stall frame engine shed at Drumheller, Alberta, all three of which were served by a wye track; none of these places had any maintenance facilities whatsoever. Yet another 2-stall engine shed, with no maintenance facilities, was located on the CNoR at Belmont, Manitoba. At Bancroft, Ontario, the CNoR had a 1-stall engine shed of frame construction, originally put up by the Central Ontario Railway, which was absorbed by the Canadian Northern between 1909 and 1914.[24]

The following three structures are of sufficient size to be described as engine houses, rather than sheds, and were built within a 15-year period and representative of the alternative to the small roundhouse, albeit little resorted to on Canadian roads.

The first of these, in a sense, hardly belongs in a strictly Canadian study, but inasmuch as it was built in Canada, it is included. In 1927-28 the Père Marquette Railway, subsequently taken over by the Chesapeake & Ohio, built a 4-stall rectangular engine house at Chatham, Ontario, of wood construction on a concrete foundation. The structure, with a low-pitched roof, was 90 feet in length and 93 feet 6 inches in width, and the engine pits were 65 feet in length. The two outer stalls were 20 feet in width and the two inner were 18 feet. The pitch of the roof lay across the structure, with one side wall 20 feet 4 inches in height and the other 16 feet 5 inches. A side annex, 17 feet 6 inches wide, housed the boiler room, coal room, shop and office. The annex had concrete floors and the engine house or stalls had a cinder floor.[25]

The GTR's Report of the Locomotive and Car Department 1919 describes a rectangular engine house, 250 feet in length by a little under 61 in width, at Lindsay, Ontario. This was a 4-track, of which two were run-through and two stub track. The engine house was built of brick, with accommodation for nine locomotives. A drop pit under two tracks was equipped with a hydraulic jack. The engine house included, whether in an annex or within the structure itself, a machine shop and smith shop, whose machinery was belt-driven by a horizontal steam engine. The power plant comprised two boilers and an air compressor, supplemented by stoves. Two adjacent buildings housed the carpenter's shop, casting shed and an apprentices' classroom in one, and the office, coaling facilities and sandhouse in the other. The engine house was served by a wye track rather than a turntable.[26]

In August 1942 plans were drawn up for a similarly designed engine house to be built for the CNR at Lindsay, but a notation on the plan read "not constructed as plan, 17 August 1942." This plan shows the draftsman's plans for the structure, dated 17 August 1942, but it is not known whether the engine house was ever built. In any case, as with the earlier GTR structure at Lindsay, this structure was of similar design, rectangular in shape and measuring 250 feet in length by 62 in breadth. As with the earlier engine house at this location, two of the tracks offered egress at both ends, and two were stub tracks, ending in buffers. The walls were of brick and the roof is marked "ready roofing" on the plan and appears to be of wood. There were 17 windows to the side, each of which was 11 feet 8 inches wide, interspersed

---

23   Robert A. Dorman, *A Statutory History of the Steam and Electric Railways of Canada* 1836-1937, (Ottawa: King's Printer, 1938).

24   Canadian Northern Railway Co., *Encyclopaedia* CNR, (Montreal, 1918), pp. 4, 7-9.

25   Chesapeake and Ohio Historical Society, courtesy of.

26   PAC, RG36 Series 35, Vol. 23, Report of the Locomotive and Car Department, Grand Trunk Railway 1919, pp. 101-5 *passim*.

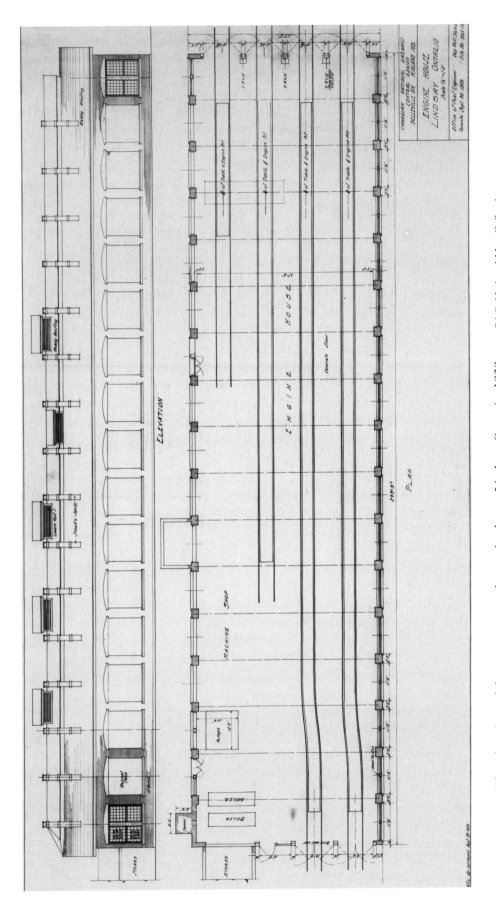

Plan drawings of the CNR rectangular engine house, Lindsay, Ontario, 1929. — PAC, National Map Collection

117

with brick pilasters 3 feet on the side and 17 inches thick. The floor was concrete. From the plan in profile, it appears that there were no fewer than 16 smoke jacks, and there were 5 louvred ventilators installed in the roof. Two boilers were installed in one corner of the engine house, although not enclosed, near which was a rectangular pump room measuring roughly 12 by 13 feet. The machine shop ranged down one side of the engine house in an open space taking up half the length of the building by reason of the stub track. A chimney 6 feet 6 inches square rose from one corner of the building, and there was a stores annex approximately 15 by 12 feet at the same corner. Judging from the drawing in side elevation, one gets the impression of a rather handsome building, but no photographs have been found, and the structure itself is no longer listed in company service — if indeed it was ever actually built. If built, it may have been sold or leased to other owners for conversion to an entirely new function.[27]

The Roberval & Saguenay Railway's engine house at Bagotville, Quebec, is designated a roundhouse on the draftsman's drawing, dated 19 November 1937, but it is fairly obvious that this is a misnomer and that the 3-stall structure was a rectangular, frame engine house, or "square house." The Bagotville engine house is no longer listed by the Roberval & Saguenay as in the company's service, and so if extant must have been converted to other use. Its overall length, including the annex, was 103 feet 4 inches and width 50 feet 5 inches. The roof sloped from a height of 23 feet at the front to 17 at the rear, and each of the three stalls was 72 feet in length. The foundation consisted of wood posts resting on timber sills with an earthen floor. The annex measured 15 feet by 17 feet 4 inches. The only other engine house to present knowledge on the Roberval & Saguenay is the roundhouse at Arvida, now used by the company as a storehouse. Whether or not this engine house in Bagotville was actually built is unknown, but in most cases a draftsman's plan is evidence of construction.[28]

Included is a reproduction of a blueprint, dated 6 April 1942, in the CNR's Montreal office, for construction of a 2-stall rectangular engine house at Barry's Bay, Ontario. The foundation consisted of 19 concrete piers, 14 inches square, carried below frost and extending 3 inches above grade. The 90-foot-long-by-40-feet-wide structure was of frame construction, with side walls 18 feet 6 inches in height, built of drop siding and shiplap, with 2-by-6-inch studs at 16-foot intervals. The roof, rising to a slight peak, was constructed of 2-inch tongue-and-groove lumber, on which was laid 4-ply felt, pitch and gravel roofing; the beams were 10-by-16-inch Douglas fir, supported by roof posts, six in number, of 10-inch square timbers. The floor consisted merely of a 6-inch bed of cinders, and the two engine pits were 72 feet in length. In all there were six windows, two on each side wall and two on the end wall, each roughly 9 by 7 feet, with nine individual panes or lights (10 inches by 12 inches) to each window. The window sills on the side walls were 6 feet above the ground. The doors were constructed of tongue-and-groove lumber. Four smoke jacks, 4 feet across the base, tapering to 1 foot 8 inches at the top, and nearly 16 feet in height, were installed in the roof. As with the Bagotville engine house, documentary evidence for the actual construction of this structure has not been found, but again it is likely that it was built.[29]

This completes our survey of Canadian engine houses, both "round" and "square," increasingly plain utilitarian structures as time went on, yet forming a part of the nation's industrial heritage.

---

27 PAC, RG30M, National Map Coll., deposit 24, item 364.
28 Roberval & Saguenay Railroad, draftsman's plan, dated 19 Nov. 1937.
29 PAC, RG30M, National Map Coll., deposit 24, item 340, draftsman's plan, dated 15 May 1942; Ibid., item 335, plan dated 6 April 1942.

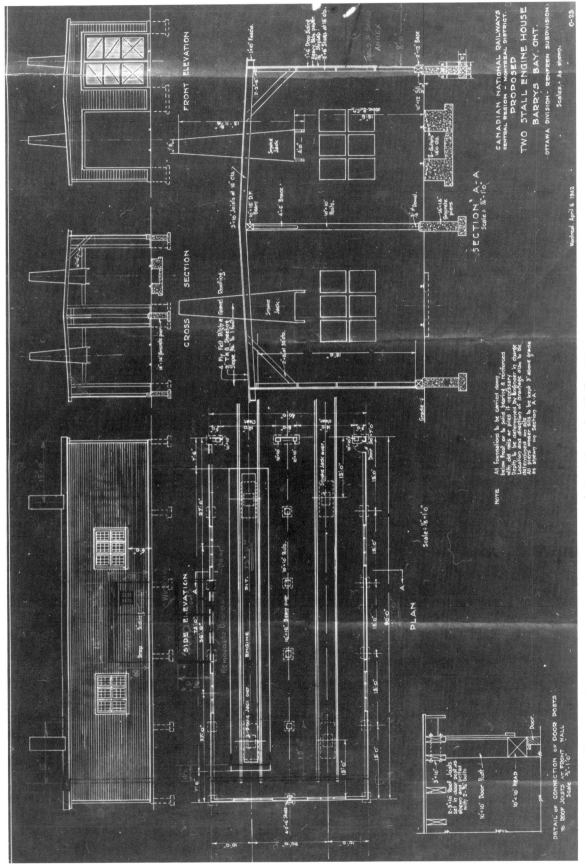

Blueprint of the proposed engine house at Barry's Bay, Ontario, 1942, CNR., – NAC, National Map Collection

CPR roundhouse and turntable at Farnham, Quebec.

The Anatomy of the Turntable

The turntable was an indispensable part of the roundhouse complex. Without it, locomotives could not be moved into or out of the stalls. Whenever a breakdown on the turntable occurred, the roundhouse was effectively blockaded. The turntable could only be dispensed with by use of the rectangular engine shed, or "square house," in conjunction with a wye track or a transfer table. A number of turntables survive today, their attendant roundhouses having long since disappeared, as for example at North Bay, Ontario. The turntable therefore merits special attention in a study of roundhouses.

Much of roundhouse technology in Canada was based on American concepts, Canadian design being primarily adaptive rather than innovative, as was the case with railway technology in general. In the course of this research only one Canadian innovation was noted: the introduction of ball bearings in place of roller bearings at the centre pivot. This occurred around the turn of the century, a few years before American designers adopted them. Even here Canadian designers were following the lead of Europeans. In all other particulars, there appears to have been little to distinguish Canadian turntables from American.

A turntable is basically a swing bridge, pivoted at the centre, or in the words of the *American Civil Engineers' Handbook* (New York, 1930), "a type of swing bridge which revolves horizontally about a vertical axis." As such, bridge terminology is used to describe turntables, and generally speaking, bridge manufacturers designed and built turntables to their clients' requirements. The turntable specifications for a particular railway depended on the type and class of locomotives in use, and in the age of steam there was a considerable range in locomotive size and weight. To meet these requirements "standard" designs were devised to keep pace with the steam locomotive. Several draftsmen's line drawings were found of standard designs for particular railway companies. Appendix O lists various Canadian turntable manufacturers based on contracts let by the Department of Railways and Canals between 1901 and 1929, chiefly for the ICR. This is obviously far from a complete listing, but indicative of the leading manufacturers in eastern Canada at that time.[1]

The reader is referred to Fig. 1 showing a typical turntable of undisclosed American manufacture dating from 1889. The part marked B B in the upper drawing is the girder or beam, designated of the plate-girder type because the girder was composed of a solid piece of iron or steel with vertical pieces known as stiffeners; the solid portion was the web. Fig. 3 shows an earlier design using a trussed beam, made up of individual members (in this particular case, wrought iron) so designed as to distribute stress uniformly and so give maximum strength. The plate-girder turntable, which came into universal use by the 1890s, was designed by riveting a flange along the top and lower edges of the web. A solid rectangular structure was completed with cross-loading girders, seen in the lower drawing. In this type of turntable, known as the balanced type, in general and indeed exclusive use on this continent until about 1912, the bridge structure rested on a central pivot whose bearings took the whole weight of the turntable and its load. The pivot, in turn rested on a solidly based pier of stone or concrete whose foundation extended below the frost line. C C (Fig. 1) shows the circular pit, 3 or 4 feet in depth, in the centre of which stood the pier and pivot; the floor of the pit was sloped for drainage. Around the pit wall, set below the level of the rim with the access tracks set in a radiating pattern, ran a circular track (D D, lower drawing) on which ran a one- or two-wheeled truck bolted to the under side of the main girders at either end. These wheels

---

1   Thaddeus Merriman and Thomas H. Wiggin, ed., 5th ed., *American Civil Engineers' Handbook,* (New York: John Wiley & Sons, 1930), p. 1202.

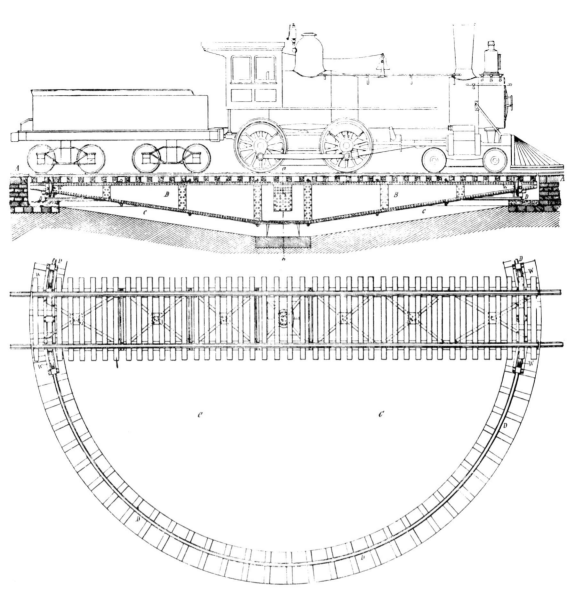

Fig. 1. Line drawing of the typical balanced turntable, 1889.

– *Railroad & Engineering Journal,* June 1889

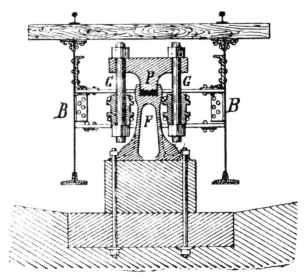

Fig. 2. Cross-sectional drawings of the centre pier and bearings, 1889.

– NAC, Barnett Collection

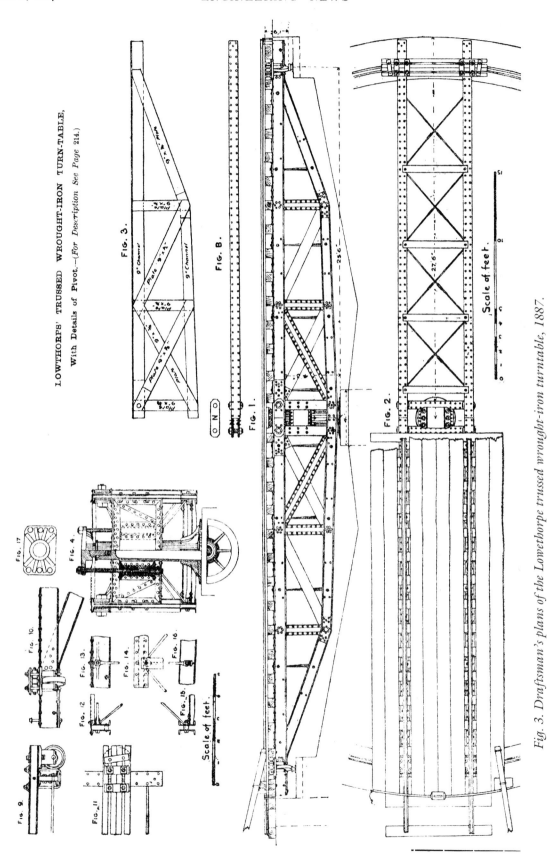

LOWTHORPS' TRUSSED WROUGHT-IRON TURN-TABLE,
With Details of Pivot.—(*For Description See Page 214.*)

Fig. 3. Draftsman's plans of the Lowethorpe trussed wrought-iron turntable, 1887.
— NRC, *Engineering News*, 2 April 1887

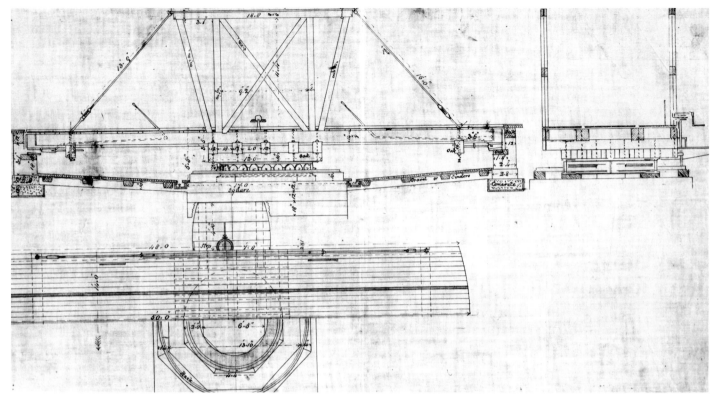

Fig. 4. Drawings of the trussed superstructure turntables on GTR, proposed for Toronto and Brock-
ville, 1853. — NAC, Barnett Collection

Half-through-type turntable, CNR, Trenton, Ontario, n.d. — CNR Archives

came into operation only to take the weight of locomotives moving on or off the turntable. Once the locomotive and tender were precisely balanced, the turntable operated freely on its centre pivot only, the wheels riding clear of the circular track. This reduced friction to a minimum so that the early turntables, if well designed and maintained, could easily be turned by one man. The turntable track was laid on ties or sleepers set on the turntable so as to align perfectly with the radiating tracks which the turntable served. The top drawing (Fig. 1) shows in profile the pit wall, of rubble or concrete construction. Obviously the ease with which the turntable could be operated depended upon the centre bearings and pivot, whose design must reduce friction to a minimum. Fig. 2 shows in cross-section the centre pier and bearings. P is the pivot, F the vertical post, fitted at the end with a cast-iron or steel bearing, and G G bolts taking the entire weight of turntable and load. By slacking off on these bolts, the turntable could be lowered to rest on the circular rail, the centre cap removed, and access gained to the bearings for maintenance. There were two types of bearings in use, about which more will be said later. For the present these may be cited as the roller-bearing and the disc-bearing types. In the latter, which is apparently the type depicted, two well-lubricated discs in contact facilitated easy rotation, whereas in the former, conical or roller bearings set in a race served the same function. Fig. 4 shows an early 1850s turntable in use on the GTR using roller bearings set in a race.[2]

A study of turntables in North America falls into two sharply defined stages. Until the introduction of the three-point or rim turntable about 1912, the centre-balanced turntable was used exclusively on this continent. In the centre-balanced type, all the weight was taken on the centre bearings with the load balanced thereon, the ends of the turntable swinging free. The three-point or rim turntable took the weight of the structure and load at three points, viz., the trucks at either end of the structure and on the central pier, distributed evenly. There were two types of rim turntables, the continuous span and the twin girder, the latter of which seems to have been generally used in Canada. The balanced-beam type continued in service in many places in Canada after 1912, but new turntables for heavy duty were of the three-point type.

To complete the anatomy of the turntable, three basic designs derived from bridge construction must be described. These designs were the deck bridge, through bridge and half-through bridge design, into one category or another of which all turntables fall. In the deck bridge type, the sleepers and rails are supported on or very near the top chord of the girders or trusses. The design is well illustrated in Fig. 1 and many of the early turntables were of this design. In the through bridge design the track is located on or near the lower chord of the girders, with the tops of the girders extending several feet above the rails. The half-through design is a compromise between the former two, in which the track is somewhat below the top chord of the girders, but so near the top that, in the words of the *American Civil Engineers' Handbook*, "no overhead bracing can be used." The half-through design, in which the track level is nearer the top of the girders than the bottom, is well illustrated in the photograph of a CNR turntable at Trenton, Ontario. This photograph shows in sharp detail the plate-girder design, in which the upper and lower flanges, the web and the vertical stiffeners show to effect.

THE BALANCED-BEAM TURNTABLE

Early Turntables

The earliest known turntables were of largely wood construction, 50 feet or less in length, and fitted with rack-and-pinion gearing operated by a hand-turned crank. At time of writing,

---

2   *Railroad and Engineering Journal,* June 1889, p. 285-6 (found in Barnett Coll. old Vol. 53).

the location and manufacture of the first turntable on this continent is unknown. The earliest reference to an American patentee appears in an 1853 issue of the *American Railroad Journal,* an advertisement placed by Carhart of Cleveland. His turntable, of 30 tons capacity, fitted with a hand crank and rack-and-pinion gearing, could be turned, presumably a full circle, by one man in less than a half-minute. Carhart claimed the patronage of the Hudson River Railroad, the Ohio & Pennsylvania, and several other early American roads. The centre pier and pit wall were of stone. Another early American patentee was Thomas Dunn, who took out his first patent about 1855. By 1867 Dunn was turning out from his Manchester, New Hampshire, shop, a 50-foot wrought-iron beam turntable. This description connotes a solid wrought-iron beam rather than trussed girder design, and if so, may be considered somewhat in advance of its time.[3]

The first documentation found on a Canadian turntable was one projected, probably in 1853, for installation at Brockville, and another of the same design at Toronto on the GTR. A line drawing of this turntable, with trussed superstructure, is included Fig. 4. The Brockville structure was 45 feet in length, and the Toronto turntable was 50 feet. The concrete centre pier measured 17 feet square. The pit was laid with gravel or cinders and sloped to the centre for drainage. Although the main girders, about 16 inches thick, are not marked as such, they were probably wood. They carried the track and the superstructure, which as may be seen from the drawing was supported from either end by iron truss rods fitted with turnbuckles for adjustment of the tension. The main members of the superstructure were 8-by-8-inch beams, with diagonal 6-by-4-inch support members. The pit wall was of concrete construction, and its parapet, which supported the incoming tracks, was of oak, as was the housing for the locking device on the underside of the main girders at either end. This locking device was operated by 5-foot levers located on either side of the superstructure. Unlike later models of the balanced turntable, this one lacked wheels at the ends of the table designed to run on a single circular track mounted on the pit wall. Both these features were absent in this early GTR model which thus was supported entirely on its centre bearings. The drawing clearly shows the crank and the rack-and-pinion gearing by means of which the turntable was operated. Gearing was resorted to only in the very early turntables. The turntable rotated on a number of rollers, on which was mounted an oak drum 12 feet in diameter and 10 inches thick. Mounted around the rim of this drum, as may be seen in the drawing, were a number of oak pedestals set at 2-foot intervals, on which was set the turntable structure. Apart from the rollers, the race in which they ran, the pier, pit wall and truss rods, this turntable was constructed of wood, probably oak.[4]

According to the *Report of the Special Committee appointed to inquire and report on the condition, management and prospects of the Grand Trunk Railway Company for 1857,* there were in that year ten 50-foot turntables on the Montreal-Toronto division and five 45-foot turntables on the Toronto-Sarnia division. These GTR structures were the earliest for which documentation was found for railways in British North America — which is not to say that they were the first.[5]

Another deck-type turntable, with trussed superstructure, approved for the Prince Edward Island Railway in 1872, was of somewhat similar design to the foregoing GTR structure. It will be noted at the outset that the PEIR turntable had a simpler superstructure (known as a king-post truss) than the GTR design of 20 years earlier, probably because the

---

3   *American Railroad Journal,* (New York), 19 Feb. 1853, p. 128; PAC. MG30 B86, Barnett Coll., old Vol. 153.

4   Ibid., new Vol. 288.

5   *Report of the Special Committee appointed to inquire and report on the condition, management and prospects of the Grand Trunk Railway Co.,* (Toronto; John Lovell, 1857), p. 81.

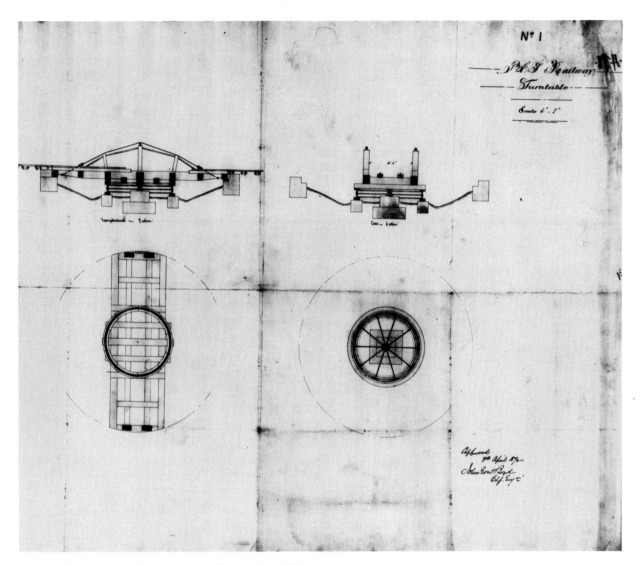

Drawings of the PEIR trussed turntable, 1872.   – NAC, National Map Collection

table proposed for the PEIR in 1872 was only 32 feet in length. Unlike the earlier GTR structure, the centre pier was mounted on three separate foundations. It would appear from the plan drawing that this turntable, too, operated by means of rack-and-pinion gearing, but there is insufficient detail in the drawings to confirm this. It must be considered a very primitive turntable, for from the 1870s turntable technology made rapid strides in both the U.S. and Canada.[6]

Plate Girders And Frictionless Bearings

Two developments marked the progress of turntable technology through the 1880s and 1890s: wholesale introduction of the solid-plate girder (deck at first, then the through and half-through designs), and the development of largely friction-free bearings to facilitate ease of rotation. Nonetheless, as turntables inevitably became longer and heavier to handle larger locomotives, manual operation became more laborious, leading late in the 1880s and 1890s to the powered turntable. One may say that by the mid-1890s the balanced-beam turntable had attained basically its final form, although it increased greatly in size and in capacity in the early years of the 20th century to keep pace with the rapidly increasing size and weight of the steam locomotive.

There were several American manufacturers of turntables in the latter 19th century who introduced progressive designs, among them C.A. Greenleaf, William Sellers of Philadelphia, and F.H. Saylor, associated with the Philadelphia Bridge Works. In 1878 Greenleaf introduced a wrought-iron turntable capable of handling a 60-ton load, and in 1882 a solid-girder gun-metal turntable. Greenleaf claimed that this design was much stronger and required less maintenance than the riveted type, presumably the trussed-girder design. In the early 1870s Sellers turned out cast-iron tables varying in length from 30 to 60 feet. Although some of his turntables were fitted with rack-and-pinion gearing, he recommended the free-swinging type, which because of his well-designed bearings could be operated easily by one man. Sellers used conical steel rollers running in a race formed by two precisely grooved steel plates. The pivot was made of the best quality cast steel. The conical roller was to be retained in centre-bearing design throughout the turntable era, although it is not known whether William Sellers was the first to introduce it on this continent. It is noteworthy that the Sellers' patented centre and bearings were in use by Canadian contractors for the ICR in the 1880s. F.H. Saylor of the Philadelphia Bridge Works introduced solid-plate wrought-iron girders in the design of deck-type turntables, 35 to 75 feet in length, patented in 1887 and 1889. These turntables were designed to handle 86-ton 2-8-0 freight locomotives. By 1893, according to *American Railroads,* a standard reference work by Walter Berg published that year, timber was obsolete in American turntable construction and found only on branch lines handling very light traffic. Cast-iron construction, although still used, had been largely displaced by wrought-iron plate-girder design, and that in turn was giving place to steel. By this date most American turntables were still hand operated, but increasingly those over 60 feet in length were powered by steam or electricity.[7]

Considering in more detail the design of centre bearings, mention has been made of the early rack-and-pinion gearing, two instances of which have been cited in Canadian practice. As early as the 1870s William Sellers patented a centre bearing consisting of a fixed and movable steel disc, grooved to form a race for a number of double-coned steel rollers, by the

---

6   PAC, RG30M, National Map Coll., deposit 22, item 478, line drawing, 8 April 1872.
7   *Railroad Gazette* (New York), 10 Feb. 1893, pp. 104-5, 184; *Railroad Gazette,* 10 Feb., 3 March, and 10 March 1893; Ibid., 3 March 1893, pp. 164 and 166, also 31 March 1893, p. 237; Ibid., 17 Oct. 1873, pp. 401-2; *Engineering News,* 21 Dec. 1889; Walter G. Berg, *American Railroads;* a reference book for railroad managers, superintendents, master mechanics, architects and students, (New York: John Wiley, 1893), p. 172.

action of which the table turned freely even under full load. Sellers' turntables were fitted with the same mechanism in the mid-1880s. In the 1880s the rival disc bearing underwent further developments but never superseded the roller-bearing design; rather the two designs evolved concurrently. F.C. Lowthorpe patented an early disc-type bearing in 1887. In Lowthorpe's design two well-lubricated steel discs or bearings operated to provide rotary motion. Another early disc-type bearing was produced in 1890 by the Chicago Forge and Bolt Company. The lower bearing was concave in shape and fashioned of phosphor bronze, and the upper bearing, fitting snugly, of steel. Two years later the Passaic Rolling Mill, Paterson, New Jersey, advertised steel centre bearings of ample surface to facilitate operation. The mill claimed their bearings were in use on 42 railroads. The hardened-steel discs came in 6-inch-diameter sizes for smaller tables and 7-inch for larger. Meantime Greenleaf stuck with the alternative roller bearings, made up of 16 conical roller bearings made of hardened tool steel, operating smoothly and with minimum friction between the upper and lower housings. Still, with the increase in locomotive size and weight by the 1890s something more was needed.[8]

The answer to this was power. The first powered turntables were driven by steam. In 1885 a brochure issued by the William Sellers Company of Philadelphia advertised a steam-powered turntable on which was vertically mounted a boiler and engine. Two years later Pennsylvania Railway's Meadows Shop, near Jersey City, built a steam-powered turntable; the boiler was vertically mounted and the engine operated on an 8-inch cylinder producing 5 horsepower. The turntable could make a complete revolution in 25 seconds. By 1892 the PRR had two more such turntables, a 60-foot table at Camden, New Jersey, and a second of 70 feet in West Philadelphia. In 1889 John D. Bowman, mechanical engineer with the PRR, patented a rival system using compressed air, produced by an air compressor in the roundhouse complex. Bowman's air motor could rotate the turntable in either direction with equal facility. Air motors would far outlast steam, and probably as many of Canada's surviving turntables are air-driven as are electric. In 1903 the American Bridge Company, Trenton, New Jersey, introduced a high-speed compressed-air tractor operating on 80 pounds air pressure and capable of turning its 75-foot turntable with 155-ton loads through a complete revolution in only a minute and a half. Electrical power was preferred by many railroad engineers where readily available.[9]

The origins of the electrically-driven turntable are vague. One issue of *Railroad Gazette* credits German engineers with devising the first, about 1890, and another issue states that one had been designed and built in 1890 by the Yale and Towne Manufacturing Company, Stamford, Connecticut, and that such tables were in service with the Pennsylvania, Philadelphia & Reading, the Chicago, Burlington & Quincy, and the Wisconsin Central railways. *Central Engineer, Car Builder and Railroad Journal* credited the first electrically-driven turntable to the West Milwaukee roundhouse on the Chicago, Milwaukee & St. Paul Railway in 1897. Hence research to date has not determined by whom or where the first electric turntable was devised. If in Germany, it must have been very early in 1890 or 1889. The Chicago, Milwaukee & St. Paul's turntable, powered by a 10-horse motor, could make a complete revolution with a 4-6-0 locomotive in 45 seconds. The manufacturer of the motor was the Gibbs Electrical Company, Milwaukee.

---

8   PAC. MG30, B86, Barnett Coll., Vol. 288, file no. 3: *Engineering News-Record*, (New York: *Engineering News-Record*, (New York: Engineering News Publishing, 1887), 2 April 1887, pp. 214-5; *Railroad Gazette*, 28 Feb. 1890; Ibid., 5 Feb. 1893, p. 101; Ibid., 10 March 1893, pp. 184-5.

9   PAC. MG30, B86, Vol. 288, Barnett Coll., brochure William Sellers and Co., Philadelphia 1885; *Railway Review*, 26 Nov. 1887; *Railroad Gazette*, 16 Sept. 1892; Ibid., 14 June 1889; Ibid., 17 April 1903, pp. 282-3.

By 1903 the General Electric Company had introduced a 10-horsepower direct-current motor, enclosed in a waterproof and dust-proof casing of cast-iron, for which several advantages were claimed over steam, including more economical operation, since power was consumed only when the table was in operation, inexpensive maintenance, and excellent speed control. Current was supplied either through trolley wires around the pit wall, by collector rings and brushes at the centre of the table, or by the same arrangement overhead, which seems to have been the commonly used method in Canada. Hand-operated turntables were not completely supplanted — a few are extant today, such as the one at Wakefield, Quebec (originally from Kingston, Ontario) — but they were of necessity relegated as time went on to branch lines with light traffic.[10]

Before turning to the Canadian scene, it may be helpful to touch briefly on American railroaders' consensus on turntable development early in the 20th century, when the balanced-beam turntable had reached its peak, shortly to be superseded for heavier duty by a new design. In the main, Canadian development paralleled American development, although slower paced.

In 1912 the American Railway Bridge and Building Association conducted a survey of 57 railroads on this continent, which included the principal Canadian roads. Although the deck-plate girder was reported the most popular, the heavier loads and longer spans called for thicker girders, less subject to deflection, which had introduced the through and the half-through plate-girder designs. The former was reported as standard equipment on seven railroads, including the Canadian Intercolonial and Grand Trunk roads. Standards called for a maximum permissible deflection of one-half inch fully loaded. The ever-lengthening tables demanded deep girders. Fully loaded the ends of the table must clear the circle rail and the table swing free on its centre pivot. Both roller bearings using conical rollers and disc bearings were used. Opinion was divided among railroad men on the respective merits of these methods. Disc centres were cheaper to install than roller bearings, but some railroaders contended that disc bearings were more trouble prone, and in any case, roller bearings were the more widely used. Electrical power was the most popular. Air motors were widely used, although some roads reported malfunctioning in severe cold (which has not restricted their use in Canada). Gasoline tractors were used on some railways, but were less favoured because of the fire hazards. By 1912 steam-driven turntables were few in number, indeed relics of the past. Concrete construction was almost universal for pier foundations and circle walls, although cut stone and even timber were to be found. Circular rail was generally laid on short wooden ties, wholly or partially embedded in concrete; sometimes the rail was secured by shoes or tie plates, as were approach rails on the parapet of the turntable pit, and timber 8 inches thick and 12 wide was recommended at this point to cushion the ends of the radiating rails in order to absorb the shock of locomotives moving on and off the turntable. Such then was the consensus among American and Canadian railroaders in 1912, on the eve of a breakthrough in turntable technology.[11]

Canadian Balanced-beam Turntables

Manufacturers.
With this background in turntable technology over the 60-odd years that the balanced-beam design was used exclusively in North America, one may turn to the Canadian scene. Herein documentation is scattered, although there are many draftsmen's line drawings showing considerable detail of a technical nature. Several of these have been selected as being compre-

10 *Railroad Gazette,* 4 March 1892; Ibid., 14 March 1890; *American Engineer, Car Builder and Railroad Journal,* June 1897; *Railroad Gazette,* 13 Nov. 1903, p. 813.
11 *Engineering News,* 5 Dec. 1912, pp. 1058-61; Ibid., p. 1059-60.

hensible to the general reader in following the evolution of the turntable from the 1880s to the close of the First World War.

An introductory word should be said about manufacturers. These were bridge manufacturers, as the names of the two principal firms, Dominion Bridge and Canadian Bridge, denote. Canadian railways did not necessarily restrict themselves to Canadian firms, although a government-owned road such as the ICR and later CNR would be expected to deal with Canadian companies. The Algoma Central & Hudson Bay Railway dealt with an American firm for its Sault Ste. Marie terminal. As mentioned in a previous context, the railway companies did not build their own turntables, but let contracts to various firms, the principal one of which undoubtedly was the Dominion Bridge Company in Lachine, Quebec. Another active company in the field was Canadian Bridge of Walkerville, Ontario, now defunct for a number of years. To these may be added the Canada Foundry Company of Toronto and the Hamilton Bridge Works of Hamilton, Ontario. The former took out a number, and perhaps all, of the contracts for the T&NO (Temiskaming & Northern Ontario Railway, now known as the Ontario Northland or ONR). By virtue of the Railways and Canals Department records, our documentation is rather heavily weighted on the ICR, which dealt before the turn of the century with the Maritime firms of William Hazlehurst, foundryman of Saint John, New Brunswick, William P. McNeil and Company, New Glasgow, Nova Scotia (who filled a number of ICR contracts well into the early years of the 20th century), D.R. and R.H. Morrison, Carleton Point, Prince Edward Island, and also the Quebec firm of Carrier Laine, Lévis. In 1890 the G.J. Brown Manufacturing Company, Belleville, Ontario, filled a contract for the Northern Pacific & Manitoba Railway at its Winnipeg terminal. In 1918 a Winnipeg firm, the Manitoba Bridge and Iron Works, took some CNR contracts. To these may be added Matheson and Company, Amherst, Nova Scotia, and the Structural Steel Company, Montreal. All these companies were active in the early years of the century.[12]

Structural Development.

Canadian railways converted from wooden to iron turntables in large measure in the 1870s and 1880s, with the early cast-iron tables giving place to wrought iron. Rough notes for the railway sessional papers indicate that the Toronto & Nipissing Railway had a 40-foot iron turntable in the 1870s. In 1879 the CPR replaced their 40-foot wooden turntable at Selkirk, Manitoba, with a 50-foot iron table, this length being set as the minimum for construction. On the ICR cast-iron turntables were installed in 1878-79 at Saint John, New Brunswick, and at Rivière du Loup, Quebec. In May 1879 the ICR let contracts to William Hazlehurst, Saint John, for replacement of their wooden turntables with iron ones, for $790 each, at four points: Ste. Flavie, Quebec; Campbellton and Newcastle, New Brunswick; and Truro, Nova Scotia. Specifications called for the same design as those installed at Halifax and Saint John; castings were to be of "good grey iron, with an admixture of scrap," to produce tough castings without brittleness, and wrought iron was to be used for bolts and wedges. The bearings were to turn on conical rollers of cast steel in a grooved circle or race. In March 1880 William Hazlehurst took four more contracts for the ICR with the Department of Railways and Canals, for a total payment of $2,600. Two of the cast-iron tables were to be of 50 feet length and two of only 30 feet, to be completed and installed by 30 June 1880. In October 1884 the ICR let contracts to the Lévis, Quebec, firm of Carrier Laine and Company for two wrought-iron turntables, 52 feet in length, to be installed at Rivière-du-Loup and Ste. Flavie, Quebec, by Christmas Day, at a cost of $1,370 each. The specifications called for "wrought iron arms" (leading to the surmise that these were trussed rather than solid-beam girders) and the Sellers patented

---

12 *Manufacturers' List Buyers' Guide of Canada* 1904, (Montreal: Manufacturers' List Co., 1904), p. 476.

centre bearing enclosed in a cast-iron box. Conical steel rollers ran in a race formed with two steel plates. On the face of it, the two turntables supplied by Carrier Laine for Ste. Flavie and Rivière-du-Loup in 1884 seem to have replaced, after a short interval, those contracted for by William Hazelhurst in 1878-79 for the same locations. Whether Hazelhurst completed his contract or not, or whether the Department of Railways found them unsatisfactory, is not known. Nonetheless, contracts for the turntables were let in this manner. The ICR replaced its last wooden turntable with one of cast iron at Point du Chêne during the 1883-84 season. Wooden turntables survived on a few branch lines as late as 1913 and perhaps later. A 48-foot turntable of southern pine was in use and reported in good condition on the York & Carleton Railroad at a locality called Cross Creek, a branch line connecting with the ICR in that year. The Elgin & Havelock line, connecting with the ICR, operated a timber turntable at Havelock, New Brunswick, and yet another 50 feet in length was to be found in service at Buctouche, New Brunswick, on the Moncton & Buctouche branch line, making connection with the ICR at Moncton in 1913. Obsolete equipment still served in out-of-the-way terminals on branch lines, where traffic was light.[13]

A date of transition from the trussed to the solid girder in Canadian turntable design has not been determined with any degree of precision, but the decade of the 1880s is a fair surmise. An early deck-type solid-girder turntable designed in 1889 for the Ontario & Quebec Railway (leased to the CPR in 1883) may be taken as an example of an early plate-girder type of turntable, illustrated by the line drawing produced in the company's Toronto office in November 1889. The reader is directed to the profile drawing, illustrating clearly the design of this 64-foot deck table. It will be noted that the track runs on top of the structure, or in engineering terms, along the top chord, and that the whole weight rests on the central pier, as was true of all Canadian turntables until the 1920s. Deck-type tables are still in use today, although as we shall see the through and half-through type became increasingly popular because of increasing length and heavier loads after the turn of the century. Referring to the profile drawing of the PEIR table, it may be observed that the centre pier rested on a concrete foundation, on which was constructed what appears to be a brick or masonry structure, rectangular in shape and measuring 5 feet 6 inches on the side. The foundations of the pier or pedestal extend about 5 feet below ground. The circular wall was built of the same material, to a depth of 3 feet 9 inches below grade. The pit floor was sloped for drainage about two thirds of the distance from the circular wall to the centre pier, when it then assumed an up grade to lie flush with the top of the pier. The 64-foot-3-inch plate girder was fish-bellied, with flat upper chord and taper towards the ends of the lower; the girder tapered from a thickness of 4 feet 10 inches at the centre to less than a third that at either end. Each girder had 10 vertical stiffeners. The ends of the turntable were fitted with a two-wheel truck to run on the circular track until the load had been balanced, when the whole structure would turn free on its centre bearings. No further detail is shown nor is it indicated whether this table was of wrought iron or steel.

The advent of steel in Canadian turntable construction may be noted at least as early as 1890. In that year G.J. Brown Manufacturing Company, a Belleville, Ontario, concern,

13 PAC. RG12, Department of Transport records, Vol. 1913, file 3306-7, part 1, No. 19809; Ontario Archives. RG8 1-7-B-3, box 7, Railway Sessional Papers, file Toronto and Nipissing Railroad, no. 3 rough notes; *Annual Report Minister of Railways and Canals*, 1878-9, (Ottawa: Maclean Roger, 1880), p. 8; PAC. RG43 C, Railways and Canals records, Vol. 24, no. 5879; *Annual Report Minister of Railways and Canals* 1883-4, (Ottawa: Maclean Roger, 1885), Appendix 4, p. 26; PAC. RG43 C, Department Railways and Canals records, Vol. 28, no. 7695; Ibid., Vol. 29, No. 8343; Canada. Parliament. House of Commons, Data on Various Branch Lines connecting with Intercolonial Railway 1913, pp. 17, 46, 58.

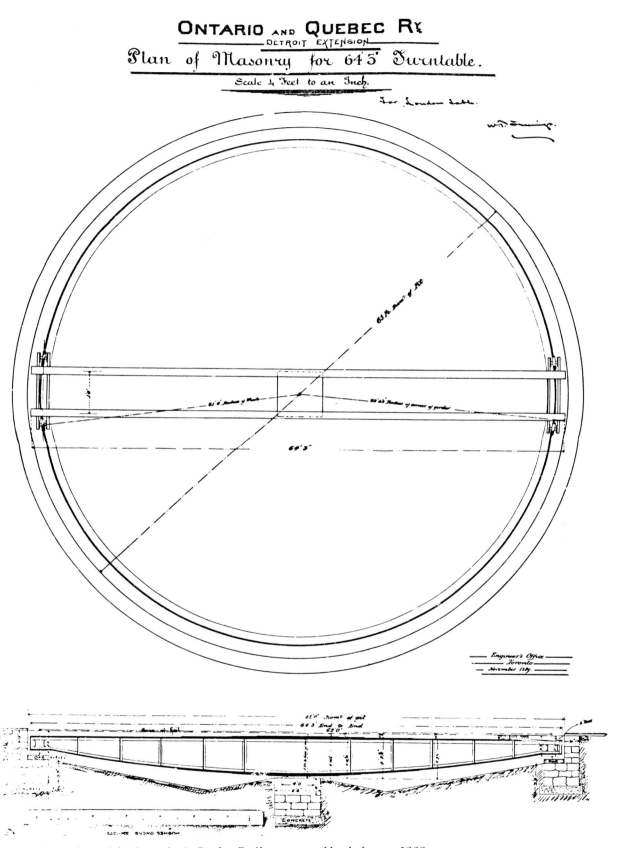

Drawings of the Ontario & Quebec Railway turntable, deck-type, 1889.

– CPR, Mechanical Dept., Montreal

contracted for two steel turntables for the North Pacific & Manitoba Railroad's Winnipeg terminal. In 1898 the Department of Railways and Canals let a contract to the Dominion Bridge Company for a 55-foot wrought-iron or medium-steel turntable, with no plate less than three eighths of an inch thick, for installation at the ICR terminal, Dartmouth, Nova Scotia, by August 31.[14]

Although the date of the first through, or half-through, plate-girder turntable in Canada is not known, there is evidence that the type was being introduced by 1900. Dominion Bridge of Lachine supplied 70-foot half-through designs for both the Canadian Pacific and the Canadian Northern railways. The CPR draftsman's line drawing dated 1900 shows the foundations for a 70-foot through turntable. Little detail, beyond the configuration, is shown for the table itself. The track level was positioned midway between the top and bottom chords, which had a slight taper from the centre to the ends. The pit floor was sloped for a distance of 30 feet from the centre for drainage. The centre pier was 8 feet square at its bottom level and tiered at two levels above that. The circular pit wall was 5 feet 9 inches thick at the base, narrowing to 4 feet 9 inches up to the ledge supporting the circular track. Also in 1900 Dominion Bridge took out a contract for the GTR, calling for a 60-foot half-through turntable.[15]

The Canadian Bridge Company, Walkerville, Ontario, contracted for a 75-foot half-through table on order by the Grand Trunk Pacific in 1907, for which a drawing Fig. 5 is provided. A turning lever at either end indicates that this turntable was unpowered, and the position of the track level about two thirds of the distance between the bottom and the top chord that the type may be described as half-through. The 75-foot turntable operated in a pit of 75 feet 6 inches diameter. The plate girders had a flat top chord and a very gently fish-bellied one on the lower, tapering slightly from a depth of slightly over 6 feet at the centre to 4 feet 8 inches at the ends. Width of the table was 13 feet 1 inch from centre to centre of the girders, or 12 feet clear width between the girders. The middle drawing shows in plan view the lateral supports and tie rods. Either end of the turntable was fitted with four end rollers, designed to clear the circular pit track by about an inch when the table was loaded and balanced. The drawings show nothing of the bearings, but the centre pier rested on a foundation 5 feet 6 inches square. The circle wall beneath the ends of the table, on which the circular track was laid, was 3 feet 6 inches thick, and the outer wall supporting the parapet of the approach tracks about 14 inches thick. Construction of the girders and lateral supports was of medium steel. By comparison consider another product of Canadian Bridge, an 88-foot-6-inch half-through model built for the Grand Trunk Pacific in 1913, this one powered by air motor. (Fig. 6) This table was designed to handle the heavy 2-8-2 Mikado freight locomotive with tender. The main girders appear of similar configuration to the one built by Canadian Bridge for the GTPR in 1907. Some data for the 1913 turntable is included on the plan, to the effect that the weight of the table was 98,000 pounds, of the centre 8,000, and the air motor 2,000 pounds, for a total of 108,000 pounds.[16]

Centre Bearings.

It will be recalled that by the 1890s the roller bearing and the disc bearing were the two designs in use on this continent, of which the conical roller bearing was favoured. For a detailed study of the roller bearing in use at this time, the reader is referred to Fig. 7 which shows the centre pivot for a turntable ordered by the ICR for installation at Saint John, New Brunswick in 1901. The conical rollers are clearly shown between the upper and lower plates,

14 *Railroad Gazette* 1890, 18 July 1890, p. 513; PAC, RG43 C, Department Railways and Canals records, Vol. 34, No. 12556.
15 Dominion Bridge Co., Lachine, draftsman's plan, dated 28 June 1900.
16 Canadian Bridge Co., Walkerville, draftsman's plan, dated 20 Aug. 1907.

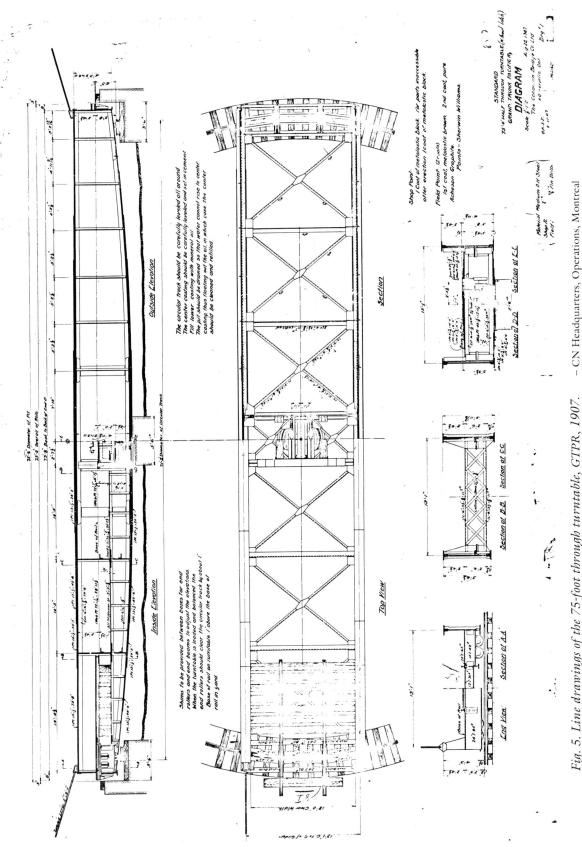

Fig. 5. Line drawings of the 75-foot through turntable, GTPR, 1907.   – CN Headquarters, Operations, Montreal

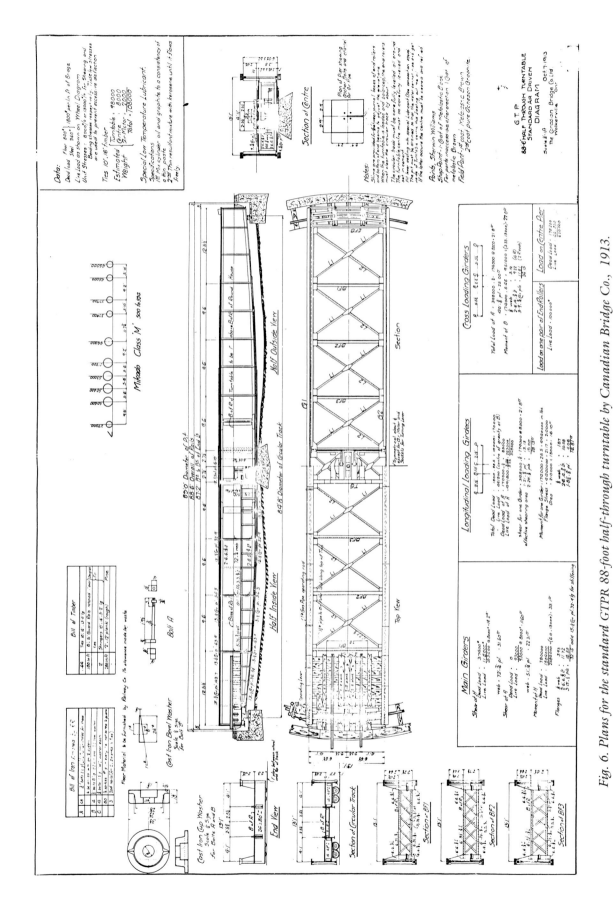

Fig. 6. Plans for the standard GTPR 88-foot half-through turntable by Canadian Bridge Co., 1913.

— CN Headquarters, Operations, Montreal

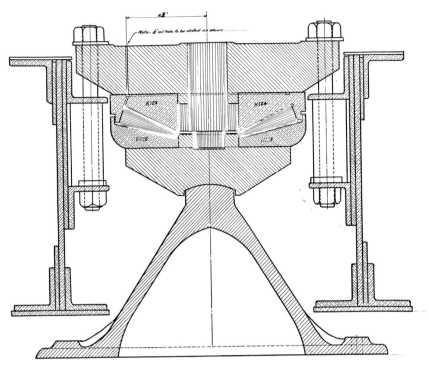

Section of ₵ of Turntable showing location of new centre.

Fig. 7. Cross-sectional drawings of the centre bearings for ICR turntable by Hamilton Bridge Works, 1901.
– CN Headquarters, Operations, Montreal

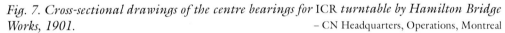
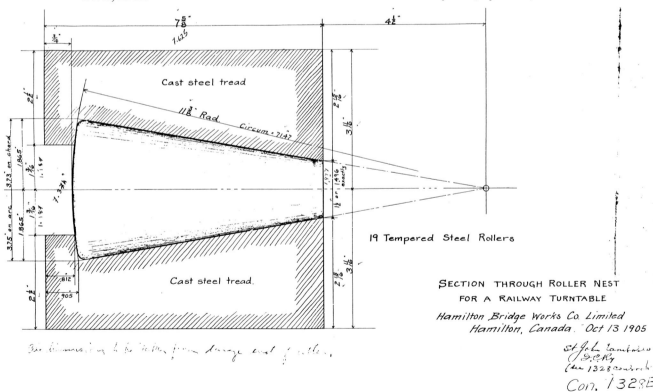

Cast steel tread

11⅜" Rad.   Circum. = 7.147

19 Tempered Steel Rollers

Cast steel tread.

SECTION THROUGH ROLLER NEST
FOR A RAILWAY TURNTABLE

Hamilton Bridge Works Co. Limited
Hamilton, Canada.   Oct 13 1905

Con. 1328E

Fig. 8. Cross-section of the roller bearings, Hamilton Bridge Works, 1905.
– CN Headquarters, Operations, Montreal

by means of which the pivot revolves. The number of roller bearings is not indicated on this cross-sectional drawing, but there were undoubtedly more than two. The adjusting screws are shown, by means of which the table could be lowered to rest upon its trucks on the circular track, enabling the top casting to be removed for maintenance work. A more detailed view of the bearings is shown in Fig. 8. Herein 19 tempered-steel conical rollers ran in a race between cast-steel plates, or treads, as shown in the drawing. The length of the rollers was 12.125 inches, and the diameter (along the chord, or straight through) was 3.73 inches. The roller nest, as designated on the drawing, measured approximately 7.5 inches square.

On foreign railways the ball bearing had come into use, a design which attracted little attention from American engineers until 1914. The *Railway Age Gazette* issue of June 1914 stated that ball bearings had been in use since 1911 on the Victoria State Railroad, Australia, and *Railway Mechanical Engineer* implied that this design was being introduced in the U.S. by 1920. In this one respect, Canadian engineers apparently led their American confrères. An April 1900 issue of *Railway and Shipping World* cited the installation of 65-foot ball-bearing-equipped turntables at a number of points on the Intercolonial. The same year, the Dominion Bridge Company supplied the CPR with a 70-foot turntable equipped with ball bearings, running on 2-inch-diameter steel balls between steel treads. By 1910 Dominion Bridge had patented a ball-bearing centre. A 70-foot turntable equipped with ball bearings is shown as a product of Toronto's Canada Foundry Company. Fig. 9 depicts how 111 two-inch steel ball bearings were cupped in countersunk spherical depressions $1\frac{1}{2}$ inches in diameter on the inner side of the plate, in which the ball bearing rotated freely. Ball bearings, however, never displaced either roller or disc bearings in Canada, as may be seen from a line drawing prepared in the drafting office of Canada Foundry in 1911. This was standard 70-foot turntable, fitted with wheel bearings, on order for the Canadian Northern Railway.[17] (Fig. 10)

Post-1918 Development of the Balanced-Beam Type.

By 1918, the year in which the Canadian Northern was taken over by the government to form part of the Canadian National Railways system, five manufacturers were catering to the needs of the newly formed government-owned railway for their turntable requirements: Canadian Bridge, Walkerville, Ontario; Dominion Bridge, Montreal and Winnipeg; the Hamilton Bridge Works, Hamilton, Ontario; the Manitoba Bridge and Iron Works, Winnipeg; and Canadian Allis Chalmers Ltd., Toronto. One order placed with Dominion Bridge on 20 June 1918 called for three 86-foot turntables, at an aggregate cost of $32,250, to be delivered within four months. In addition to the above, several other manufacturers flourished in the earlier years of the century. Canada Foundry secured a number of early contracts with the T&NO, including one with a ball-bearing centre for North Bay in 1910, a 75-foot through table for the T&NO Cochrane terminal in 1909, and a 70-foot half-through type for Canadian Northern's Winnipeg terminal in 1911. The firm of W.P. McNeil and Company, New Glasgow, Nova Scotia, filled contracts for the ICR in 1907 and 1910, and Canadian Bridge

---

17 *Railway Age Gazette,* mechanical edition (New York: Simmons-Boardman), June 1914, p. 329; *Railway Mechanical Engineer,* May 1920, p. 301; *Railway and Shipping World,* (Toronto), April 1900, p. 112; PAC. RG2 series 1, Privy Council records, 26 Sept. 1910, No. 1873, see also 22 Dec. 1910, No. 2553; Dominion Bridge, drawing 19 Jan. 1900; Canadian Foundry Co. drawing, dated 9 June 1909. Opinion among railroaders remained divided on the relative merits of the disc and roller bearing centres. *Railway Maintenance Engineer* in a 1919 issue opined that the disc centre offered simplicity of construction and ease of assembly, whereas the roller centre was more complex but easier riding. The disc type lasted a long time under continuous service, requiring comparatively little maintenance, whereas the roller centres operated more smoothly and easily when new, but required more inspection and maintenance to keep them in prime order.

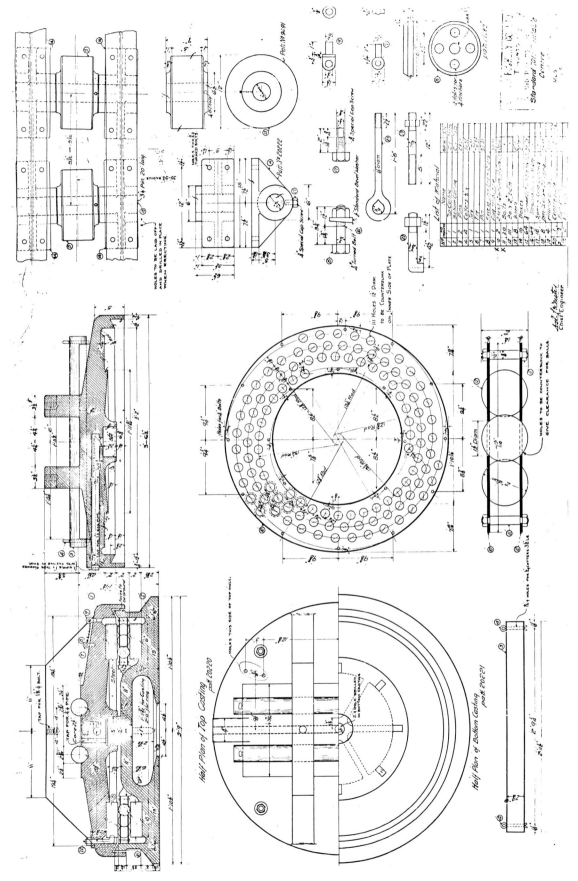

Fig. 9. Draftsman's drawings of the centre bearings for the standard 70-foot turntable, Canada Foundry Co., 1909.

—CN Headquarters, Operations, Montreal

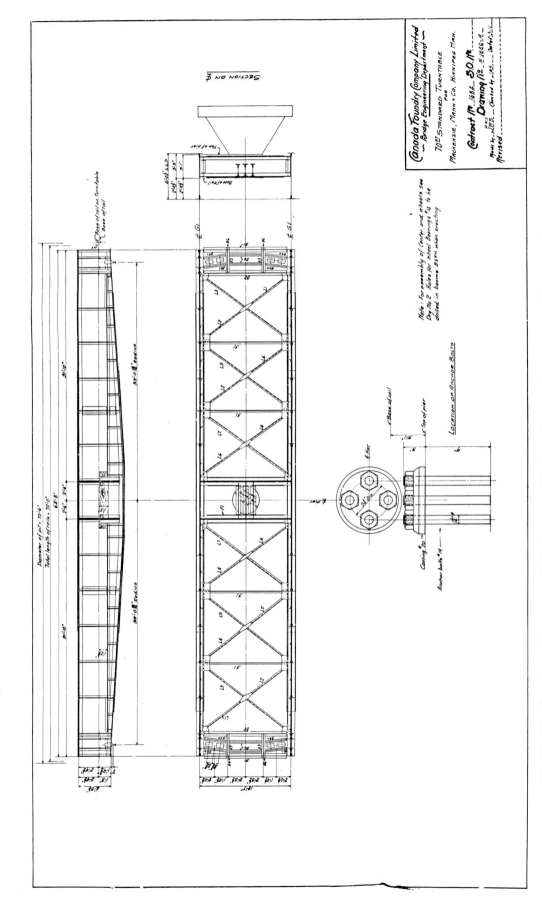

Fig. 10. Line drawings of the standard 70-foot turntable, Canada Foundry Co., ordered by CNoR in 1911.

— CN Headquarters, Operations, Montreal

of Walkerville built a 90-foot turntable for the T&NO, for installation at Timmins, Ontario, as late as 1936.[18]

Before leaving the balanced turntable, it may be of interest to note the stage it had reached before the debut of the twin-span in 1920. As early as 1905 a 100-foot turntable had been built for the GTR and installed at its Turcot (Montreal) roundhouse. This turntable was of unprecedented size in Canada.

By 1914 the standard CPR turntable was a 70-foot half-deck type with a concrete pier a little over 5 feet square carried to 6 feet below ground, and with the pit floor covered with 4 inches of broken stone or gravel. The pit wall was 5 feet 9 inches thick at its base, and the coping was oak or Douglas fir. Five years later the 90-foot half deck (by which is probably meant half-through) was designated the CPR standard. The centre pier was built of reinforced concrete, whose foundation extended 7 feet below grade, and if required, mounted on cedar piles, likewise the pit wall, on which the 85-pound-per-yard circular rail set, rested on piles at 3-foot intervals when the calculated weight exceeded $2\frac{1}{2}$ tons per square foot. A rim or parapet of oak or Douglas fir, 4 inches thick, cushioned the approach rails and took the shock of locomotives moving on and off the turntables. On the National Transcontinental in 1914 the standard turntable was a 75-foot half-through plate girder, with capacity for a 200-ton load. In 1918 Canadian Government Railways (soon to become the CNR)ordered an 85-foot through-type turntable with roller bearings from Canadian Bridge for installation at Fairview, Nova Scotia, the price on delivery $14,626.50. In its closing years as a separate entity, the Canadian Northern Railway ordered from Dominion Bridge 86-foot through turntables for installation at Blue River, Kamloops and Boston Bar, British Columbia, in 1915, and for Rainy River and Atikokan, Ontario, in 1918. Foundations were of reinforced concrete and piles were called for whenever the ground was not deemed capable of supporting 5,000 pounds per square foot.[19]

Many balanced-beam turntables continued in service long after the introduction of the improved three-point, twin-span type, but during the late 1920s and early 1930s they were found to be too short and not of sufficient strength for the much heavier locomotives coming into service in these years. Turntables in the 73-to-80-foot range were lengthened to 95 feet 6 inches and were structurally strengthened to handle much heavier loads. This entailed splicing equal-length girder extensions at either end, with corresponding extensions to the floor system. When the existing circle rail was in good condition, it was retained in service, and the extended turntable cantilevered out to the newly built pit wall. On the other hand, should the old circle rail not be worth retaining, then it was replaced on the newly built wall, and the trucks and tractor motors moved out to near the end of the extended main girders. In either case the old wall was removed, but with the use of reinforced-concrete blocks and steam-powered cranes this was fairly easily managed. Indeed, in 1934 it was estimated that most turntables were not out of service more than 48 hours, at an average cost of $4,100 in the CNR's Central Region. In 1941 the Turcot turntable's original concrete circle wall —

18   Engineer's Office, CNR Regional Office, Winnipeg, file 488; Engineer's Office, ONR North Bay, file 1835-11, old section no. 1; *Eighth Annual Report T & No Railway Commission* 1902, (Toronto: King's Printer, 1910), p. 17; Canada Foundry Co., drawing dated 8 March 1911; PAC. RG2 series 1, Privy Council records, No. 1873, 26 Sept. 1910; also no. 2553, 22 Dec. 1910; Ibid., no. 1318, 10 June 1907; Engineer's Office, ONR North Bay, file 1835-7, section 1, section 2.

19   *Railway and Shipping World*, (Toronto), Dec. 1905, p. 581; British Columbia Railway Co., plan dated 26 May 1914; CPR Corporate Archives. Chief Engineer's Office, Montreal. Standard Plans 1916, and drawing D-7702, 6 March 1919; Canada. Parliament. *Sessional Papers* 1914, No. 123, exhibit 10, Report of the National Transcontinental Railway Investigating Commission 1914; PAC. RG43 Department Railways and Canals records, Vol. 612, file 19307; Engineer's Office, CNR Regional Office, Winnipeg, file K-488-1.

$4^1/2$ feet thick and 8 feet to the base of the foundations, which had deteriorated because of frost — was demolished and replaced by 25 pre-cast reinforced-concrete sections interspersed with concrete piers carried well below the frost line. The new circle rail, 100 pounds to the foot, in 33 sections, was supported on steel chairs spaced nearly 18 inches apart. The new sections were installed as the old wall was demolished. Obviously the turntable was not being lengthened, but the circle wall merely replaced. By careful management in this no doubt ticklish job, the turntable was not out of service for more than a few hours at any one time. Plank decks were always laid on the turntables, between and to either side of the rails, in the interests of safe operation. The object was to do as much work in the shop or works as possible, leaving simple assembly at the site.[20] (see page 25)

Although the balanced-beam turntables were never displaced, being lengthened and adapted to heavier service, a new design of turntable was required to meet fully the demands of the mammoth locomotives coming into service from the 1920s.

Note the extensions of the CNR turntable at Joliette, photographed in 1933. The original guide rail remains in place, although the pit wall has been expanded.   – CNR Archives

20 *Railway Engineering and Maintenance*, (New York), Sept. 1934, pp. 480-2; *Canadian Transportation*, (Toronto), Jan. 1942, pp. 7-8.

THE THREE-POINT TWIN-SPAN TURNTABLE

Unlike the balanced-beam turntable, the three-point, also known as the five-point and the rim turntable, distributed its weight, loaded or otherwise, evenly between the centre bearings and the wheels at either end of the table. Since often there were two trucks at either end, this type often was designated as the five-point turntable rather than three. Although a well-maintained balanced table could be turned by hand, often by only one man, the three-point had to be power operated.

Origins On This Continent

The origins of the three-point turntable are unknown. Suffice it to say that it was used in Europe long before it was introduced in the United States and Canada. On the face of it, this is perhaps surprising, because the prime advantage of the three-point or rim table was that it could handle heavier locomotives, and nowhere else were locomotives the size they were in the United States after the turn of the century. Nevertheless, until about 1921 American and Canadian turntables were of the balanced type. Not only could the three-point handle heavier loads, but it could do so more expeditiously, for the tedious shifting of the locomotive and tender back and forth to find the precise point of balance was unnecessary. The elimination of this operation not only saved time but allowed a shorter turntable to handle a given size of locomotive, since with the balanced turntable there must always be enough room to balance the load.

As the stresses on turntables became much greater early in this century, main girders were lengthened to accommodate the greater wheel base of the new locomotives. This demanded much thicker and heavier girders to maintain the requisite stiffness of the structure, whose tracks had to be aligned precisely with the tracks radiating from the turntables. As girders became longer, deflection at the ends became more difficult to overcome. These factors led a number of American railroads to experiment with a new design about 1912. The three-point turntable had two basic designs: the continuous-span and the twin-span. In the former balanced-beam type, the end wheels or trucks were in contact with the pit rail only when loading and unloading the turntable; once in operation, the end wheels rode clear of the track at all times. On the other hand, with the three-point turntable the end wheels or trucks were in contact with the circular rail at all times, and the weight of the turntable and load was evenly distributed between the centre pivot or bearing and the trucks at either end of the turntable. A 1912 survey conducted by the American Railway Bridge and Building Association indicated that this new design had not yet proved practical because of the considerable power requirements to operate it under load, particularly when unevenly distributed. Experience indicated that locomotives with wheelbases over 90 feet required either a three-point turntable or the provision of a wye. As early as 1908 one of the Mallet-type locomotives on the Chesapeake & Ohio had a wheelbase 108 feet in length.[21]

Up until this time the balanced or tipping table, as it was sometimes called, offered the advantage of manual operation even with quite heavy loads, providing the bearings and the circular track were well maintained. Once larger locomotives over 95 feet in length came in, however, turntables had to be powered, and the old balanced table lost its advantage of optional manual use.[22]

---

21 *Engineering News*, (New York: Hill Publishing Co.), 5 Dec. 1912, pp. 1058-9.
22 *Engineering News-Record*, (New York: McGraw-Hill), 5 June 1924, pp. 964-5. A well-designed and maintained centre bearing turntable permitted manual turning of quite heavy locomotives, but those exceeding about 95 feet in length called for powered turntables. With the era of Big Power on this continent, in the 1920s and thereafter to the end of the steam era, powered turntables became a necessity, hence the obsolescence of the older balanced-beam or "tipping" turntable.

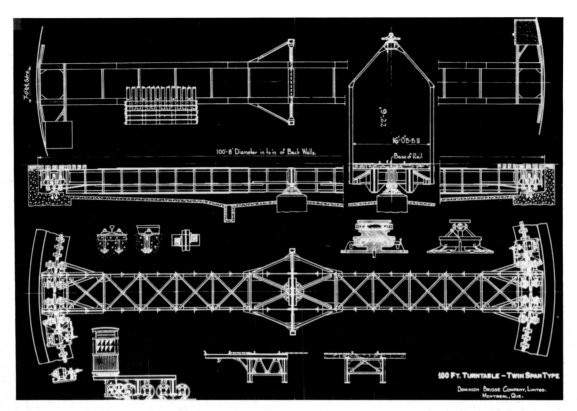

Blueprint for a 100-foot twin-span turntable, Dominion Bridge Co., 1921.

– Dominion Bridge Co., Montreal

Turntable circular rail and pit wall.

– CNR Archives

42261-7

CNR Northern #6403 rides the electrically powered turntable at Turcot in Montreal. Note the wires to the collector box above the engine. Cylinders and hose for the auxiliary air-operated turning mechanism appear in the foreground.
                                                                                                    – CNR Archives

145

The first continuous-span turntable on this continent has been credited to the American Bridge Company on order from the Wheeling & Lake Erie Railroad, installed at Cambridge, Ohio, in 1921. The alternative twin-span design was the product of the Bethlehem Steel Bridge Corporation, installed in May 1920 on the Chesapeake & Ohio Railroad. Research to date indicates that the twin-span design won general favour on Canadian roads. The continuous-span design featured lateral strength and stiffness, with flexible end trucks to equalize the load among the wheels. Each truck was separately powered. As its name denotes, the continuous-span was designed with single girders extending the full length of the turntable. The twin-span design substituted two shorter girder spans, each half the length of the turntable, connected at the centre to a transverse loading girder, mounted on the centre bearing. The twin-span girders were shallower and lighter than the continuous-span. This design allowed flexibility, with either half of the structure deflecting independently, compensating for settling and irregularities in the circular pit rail. The twin-span type was cheaper to build and to maintain.[23]

The Twin-Span Turntable In Canada
Dominion Bridge (Montreal) appears to have been the first Canadian company to introduce the twin-span turntable, about 1921. The tables were electrically, air or gasoline powered, although electricity was preferred when available. There were four equalizing trucks, two at either end of the turntable, sharing the load uniformly with the centre bearing, hence described as a five-point table. The design was closely similar to that of Bethlehem Steel previously described, even to the design of the centre bearings. A copy of a 1921 blueprint shows a draftsman's drawing of the Dominion Bridge design for their 100-foot twin-span turntable. One notices in the profile drawing the shallow girders, in contrast to the deep girders required of a balanced type of this length. The 100-foot table was 7 feet in width, and the main girders approximately $4\frac{1}{2}$ feet in uniform depth as far as the inner projection of the pit wall, where the base of the main girders is stepped up to make provision for the trucks and wheels riding on the circular rail. It will be observed that each of the two spans has six lateral girders supported by crossed members. Each span was flexibly joined to a transverse girder at the centre of the table, allowing for slight deflection. The centre bearing was of the disc type, made up of a bridge shoe unit, resting on a flat phosphor bronze disc. It was claimed that the shoe and the disc were removable for inspection and maintenance by a five-man crew in less than an hour. This whole centre unit housing the bearings was bolted beneath the transverse girders. There were two cast-steel H-shaped trucks, each mounted with a set of two standard car wheels, one wheel of which was attached to gears and powered. There were electric traction motors, one at either end mounted on structural frames, with a control cab at one end fitted with a switchboard, foot brake, and manual controls for use in case of a power failure. The figure clearly shows in longitudinal section the power arch, 16 feet wide and 22 feet 6 inches in height above the rail. At the top of the arch was the collector box connected with the power line. The collector box turned between bearings and was of necessity waterproof and positioned directly over the centre of the table. Motors were available to work off either direct or alternating current, and where electricity was not available or too expensive, air or gasoline motors could be fitted. The power collector unit was also of Dominion Bridge design. The operator sat in the control cab at one end of the table. There were 100-watt lights at each end of the turntable and two of 60 watts on each side of the

23 *Railway Review,* 29 Oct. 1921, article "Twin-Span Turntables on the Chesapeake and Ohio Railway"; *Engineering News-Record,* 5 June 1924, pp. 954-6; *Railway Maintenance Engineer,* Sept. 1919, pp. 312-4, 304.

power arch, also an interior control cab light, all of which were turned on or off from the cab.[24]

Dominion Bridge filled orders to clients' specifications, but in 1921 was marketing turntables up to 75 feet in length for loads up to 275 tons, 80-90 feet for up to 350 tons, and over 90 feet to handle locomotives exceeding 450 tons.[25]

A number of advantages were claimed for the new turntables, not least of which was a savings in length for handling equivalent loads. This is best demonstrated by reference to the next figure, comparing a deck and a half-through balanced turntable with a twin span, designed for turning the same locomotive, with an overall wheelbase of 97 feet 3 inches. Both the deck and the half-through balanced types called for a length of 123 feet 8 inches to handle such a locomotive and tender, whereas the twin-span table handled the same load with an overall length of 100 feet 8 inches, exactly 23 feet shorter. The company claimed that the twin-span turntable would turn any engine with wheel base up to one foot shorter than the length of the table itself, or a clearance of 6 inches at either end. This was obviously because balancing of the load was unnecessary, which also meant that locomotives could be turned in much less time. With the twin-span design the turntable rails and the approach rails were always closely aligned and level, so that engines could move on and off at as much as 20 miles per hour without the damaging hammer effect and end blow to which the balanced type was subject. Maintenance was easier and cheaper than with the balanced-beam type, and in addition to these advantages, the old centre foundations or piers could generally be retained from the old balanced tables for use with the new twin-spans. Finally the twin-span was easier to erect.[26]

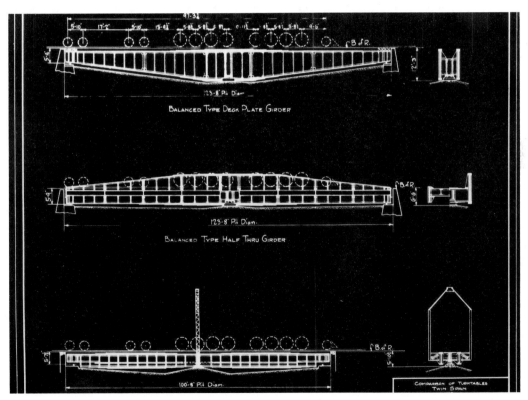

Blueprint comparing loading of balanced and twin-span turntables, Dominion Bridge Co., 1921.

– Dominion Bridge Co.

24 Dominion Bridge Co., Twin-span Turntables, Montreal 1921.
25 Ibid.
26 Ibid., *Railway Age*, 7 July 1928, p. 1.

By 1924 the Dominion Bridge Company had filled orders for six twin-spans for the CNR. In 1929 a 120-foot twin-span table was built for the new CPR John Street roundhouse. The 100-foot continuous-span turntable (the only one of this type found in Canada) supplied to the Hamilton roundhouse, TH&B railway, in 1929 came with an air motor for use as a standby, as well as an electric tractor, one mounted at each end.[27]

In 1928 the American Railway Association recommended the ideal turntable as the three-point or rim design, with minimum length 100 feet, electrically powered, and preferably of the deck type. An adequately drained concrete pit was considered best. The following year the American Bridge Company introduced Timkin roller bearings to the end trucks of its continuous-girder table, at a considerable reduction in friction. The tractor motor on one of these turntables, installed on the Southern Pacific Railway at Houston, Texas, was reduced accordingly from 25 to 15 horsepower. Furthermore, so smoothly did this turntable operate, that it was deemed that standby power could be dispensed with, since it had been demonstrated that a dozen men could turn a fully loaded table by hand. Finally, in 1938 the Merriman *American Civil Engineers' Handbook* expressed a preference for the deck-type table. By this time the days of steam on American roads were numbered, and with their passing, the need for roundhouses and their attendant turntables also gradually passed.[28]

Reference has been made in the preceding pages to the CPR's St. Luc roundhouse, built to serve the hump yard on the outskirts of Montreal West. This was the last roundhouse to be built in Canada, and possibly the last one built on this continent north of the Rio Grande. The turntable for the St. Luc roundhouse was built by the Dominion Bridge Company and was designed as a 100-foot three-point type. Unfortunately research at time of writing has adduced no further description of this turntable, which may well be taken as the culmination of railroad turntable design in Canada, but draftsman's plans procured from Dominion Bridge of a turntable designed by them in 1941 for installation at Moncton, New Brunswick, may be of interest.

The reader is referred to the figures illustrating this proposed turntable for CNR use at Moncton. The first shows the main girders in plan and profile, from which the half-through design will be noted, as well as the comparatively shallow main girder (in profile) in relation to the length, by comparison with the older balanced type. The second figure indicates that the end trucks rode on four wheels. The turntable was electrically powered, as may readily be seen by the power arch over the centre of the span and the enclosed operator's cab at one end. The final figure indicates that the centre bearings were of the disc type and were of cast steel and phosphor bronze construction.

Few if any turntables were built for railway use after dieselization, when the roundhouse itself became redundant, although some have survived as diesel shops or storage depots. Nonetheless, since both roundhouses and turntables were products of the steam area, these once familiar features of railway yards across the nation will eventually disappear.

---

27 Engineer's Office, ONR North Bay, records file 1835-11, old section no. 1; *Canadian Railway and Marine World*, (Toronto), Aug. 1929, p. 494; Engineer's Office, TH&B Railway, Hamilton, blueprint dated 30 Aug. 1929.

28 *Canadian Railway and Marine World*, Aug. 1928, p. 458; *Railway Engineering and Maintenance*, Feb. 1929, p. 77; Thaddeus Merriman, ed., *American Civil Engineers' Handbook*, (New York: John Wiley and Son, 1938), p. 2077.

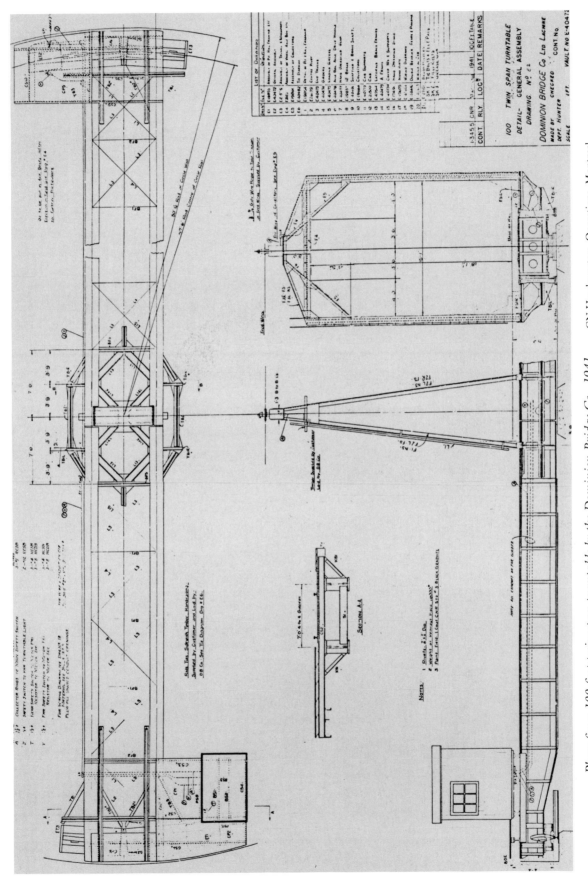

Plans for a 100-foot twin-span turntable by the Dominion Bridge Co., 1941. – CN Headquarters, Operations, Montreal

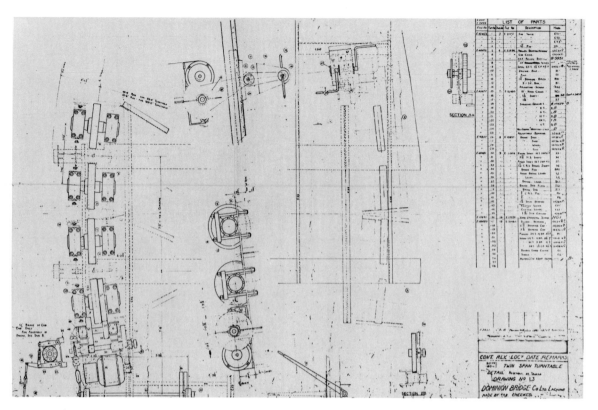

Draftsman's drawings of trucks for twin-span turntables, Dominion Bridge Co., 1941.
– CN Headquarters, Operations, Montreal

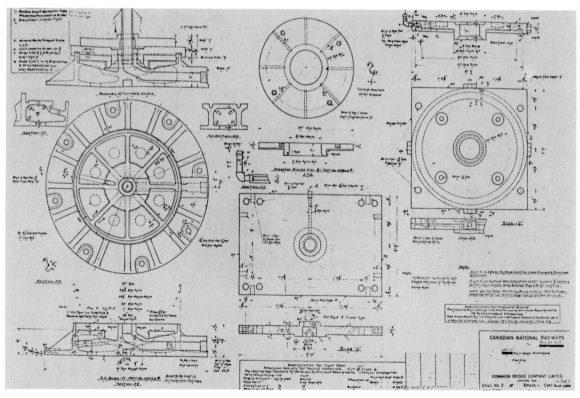

Draftsman's drawings of the centre bearings for a 100-foot twin-span turntable by Dominion Bridge, 1941.
– CN Headquarters, Operations, Montreal

Conclusion

According to current information, there are almost 70 engine houses still in service in Canada (see Appendix A), a meagre remnant indeed of the hundreds which once were to be seen in divisional yards across the nation. The roundhouse, the predominant form of engine house in North America, had been built around the steam locomotive and was found to be ill designed for the use of diesels. Some are still in service and very active, but for every survivor a score or more have been demolished. As an article published by J. Norman Lowe in *Canadian Transportation*'s June 1964 issue describes, survival has often depended on sale or lease to some commercial enterprise and conversion to an entirely new use. For example, had the Canadian Wool Growers Association not bought the CPR's Carleton Place roundhouse, one of the oldest extant in Canada, it would have been pulled down many years ago.

In his article "New Uses for Roundhouses," Lowe cites some interesting examples. The CPR roundhouse at Winyard, Saskatchewan, has been preserved but subjected to the indignity of being converted into a henhouse! By means of the addition of a second and third floor in each of its three bays, the Winyard roundhouse now serves as a chicken hatchery, turning out 5,000 chickens a year. The CNR's Prince Albert, Saskatchewan, roundhouse has been bought or leased by a brewery and serves as a storage for beer empties. A CNR roundhouse at Kamloops Junction, British Columbia, ended its days as a service garage for new automobiles. The International Block Company leased the CN's Fort Frances, Ontario, roundhouse for conversion to a plant turning out their product. In similar vein the author recalls the Trenton, Ontario, roundhouse, built in 1911 or shortly thereafter for the CNR and acquired by Trenton Glass and Window Ltd. It is now used by several commercial enterprises. In far northwestern Ontario, near the Manitoba boundary, Ontario Central Airlines acquired the CNR Redditt roundhouse, which now serves as a servicing depot for the adjacent air strip. Lowe estimates, at the time his article appeared in 1964, that fully 75 percent of the CNR's retired roundhouses had been sold or leased to various commercial enterprises for purposes very different from that for which they were built.[1]

It is hoped that restoration projects will save for posterity a sampling of these utilitarian structures. Railway stations have received much preservation attention in recent years, and our few surviving roundhouses and engine houses deserve a similar effort by the historical community.

---

1   J. Norman Lowe, "New Uses for Roundhouses," *Canadian Transportation*, June 1964.

CPR roundhouse at St. Luc yard in Montreal, built in 1949, was the last constructed in Canada.
– CP Archives

Appendix

EXTANT ENGINE HOUSES IN CANADA (Railway Service)

At the date of writing there were 67 engine houses extant in railway service in Canada, 27 of which are on the CNR, 33 on the CPR, and 7 on smaller regional lines. In addition, there are a few more sold or leased by the railway companies to various commercial firms and converted to other uses, a few of which have figured in the text. The following listings comprise engine houses still in railway service, in whole or in part.

CNR

Halifax, Nova Scotia (Fairview); Sydney, Nova Scotia; Charlottetown, Prince Edward Island; Cape Tormentine, New Brunswick; Edmunston, New Brunswick; South Devon, New Brunswick; Joffre, Quebec; Chambord, Quebec; Jonquiere, Quebec; Hornepayne, Ontario; Belleville, Ontario; Fort Erie, Ontario; Stratford, Ontario; Windsor, Ontario; Capreol, Ontario; Thunder Bay, Ontario (Neebing); London, Ontario; The Pas, Manitoba; Dauphin, Manitoba; Prince Albert, Saskatchewan; Regina, Saskatchewan; Winnipeg, Manitoba (Transcona); Winnipeg, Manitoba (East Yard); Jasper, Alberta; Hanna, Alberta (not usable); Kamloops, British Columbia; Smithers, British Columbia.

CPR

Montreal, Quebec (St. Luc Yard); Montreal, Quebec (Hochelaga, Yard); Sherbrooke, Quebec; Three Rivers, Quebec; Vallee Junction, Quebec; Megantic, Quebec; Aroostook, New Brunswick; McAdam, New Brunswick; Bay Shore, New Brunswick; Chapleau, Ontario; Sudbury, Ontario; Sault Ste. Marie, Ontario; Webbwood, Ontario; Toronto, Ontario (John Street); MacTier, Ontario; Trenton, Ontario; Smiths Falls, Ontario; London, Ontario; Windsor, Ontario; Kenora, Ontario; Minnedosa, Manitoba; Moose Jaw Saskatchewan; Sutherland, Saskatchewan; Alyth, Alberta; South Edmonton, Alberta; Medicine Hat, Alberta; Lethbridge, Alberta; Victoria, British Columbia; Coquitlam, British Columbia; Penticton, British Columbia; Revelstoke, British Columbia; Cranbrook, British Columbia; Nelson, British Columbia.

ONTARIO NORTHLAND RAILWAY (formerly Temiskaming & Northern Ontario)
Timmins, Ontario.

TORONTO, HAMILTON & BUFFALO RAILWAY
Hamilton, Ontario.

ALGOMA CENTRAL & HUDSON BAY RAILWAY
Sault Ste. Marie, Ontario.

ROBERVAL & SAGUENAY RAILWAY
Arvida, Quebec.

ESQUIMALT & NANAIMO RAILWAY
Victoria, British Columbia.

LAKE ERIE & NORTHERN & GRAND RIVER RAILWAYS
(CPR electric lines)
Preston, Ontario; Brantford, Ontario.

Sources: lists of extant engine houses supplied by the relevant railway companies.

Former Trenton roundhouse as it is today. – photo by author, 1982

Entrance to the former Carleton Place machine shop, showing semi-legible date stone above door. – photo by author, 1982

Fort Erie, Ontario, 1986.   – Greg McDonnell

CPR 15-stall roundhouse at Minnedosa, Manitoba, now used by a farm implement company, 1980.   – Greg McDonnell

Abbreviations Used

ACR   Algoma Central Railway, full title Algoma Central Hudson Bay Railway
CNR   Canadian National Railways
CNoR   Canadian Northern Railways
CPR   Canadian Pacific Railway
GTR   Grand Trunk Railway
GTPR   Grand Trunk Pacific Railway
HBR   Hudson Bay Railway
ICR   Intercolonial Railway
NTR   National Transcontinental Railway
PGE   Pacific Great Eastern Railway, subsequently British Columbia Railway
T&NO Temiskaming & Northern Ontario Railway, subsequently Ontario Northland
          Railway
TH&B   Toronto, Hamilton & Buffalo Railway

Battery-powered shop switcher (built at Stratford CN shops) for use on enclosed turntable at
Hornepayne.
                             – Greg McDonnell

Sources Cited

Notes: entries marked + have incomplete bibliographical data, which could not be supplemented from the Union List in our library.

Algoma Central and Hudson Bay Railway Co. Engineer's Office, Sault Ste. Marie, Ontario. Line drawings, plans and records.

American Engineer and Railroad Journal New York.+

American Engineer, Car Builder and Railroad Journal+

American Engineering and Railroad Journal New York.+

American Railroad Engineer.+

American Railroad Journal J.H. Schultz, New York.

American Railway Engineering Association Proceedings.+

Appleton's Dictionary of Machines, Mechanics, Engine Work and Engineering Vol. II, D. Appleton and Co., New York, 1852.

Bain, D.M. *Canadian Pacific in the Rockies,* Vol. 3, British Model Railroaders of North America, Calgary Group, Calgary, Alta., 1979.

Berg, Walter G. *American Railroads,* John Wiley and Sons, New York, 1893.

Binney, Marcus and David Pearce ed. *Railway Architecture,* Orbis Publishing Co., London, 1979.

Blackwell, Thomas E. *Report on the Grand Trunk Railway for 1859,* Waterlow and Sons, London, 1860.

British Columbia Railway Co. Vancouver, B.C., records Pacific Great Eastern Railway, line drawings photographs.

Brown, Robert R. "Ontario, Simcoe and Huron Railway," *The Railway and Locomotive Historical Society, Bulletin 85,* Railway and Locomotive Historical Society, Boston, Mass., 1952.

Canada. Department of Public Works *General Report Minister of Public Works 1873-4,* appendix 16-17, also for *1872-3,* appendices 15-17.

Canada. Department of Railway and Canals *Annual Report of the Minister of Railways and Canals 1878-9, 1879-80, 1883-4,* Maclean Roger, Ottawa.

Canada. Parliament. House of Commons *Data on various branch lines connecting with the Intercolonial Railway 1913.*

Canada. Parliament. *Sessional Papers, 1909* No. 67, *1914* No. 123, Report of the National Transcontinental Railway Investigating Commission.

Canada (Province). Parliament *Report of the Select Committee appointed to enquire and report as to the condition, management and prospects of the Grand Trunk Railway Co.,* John Lovell, Toronto, 1857.

Canada. Public Archives. MG24 D16, Buchanan Papers; MG30 B86, Barnett Engineering Coll.; RG2 Privy Council records; RG12 Department of Transport records; RG30 Canadian National Railways records; RG30M, National Map Coll., plans and drawings; RG36 series 35, Boards, Offices and Commissions records, including Report of the Locomotive and Car Departments Grand Trunk Railway 1919; RG43 Department of Railways and Canals records; RG46 Transport Commission records.

Canadian Bridge Co. Walkerville, Ont. plans and drawings.

The Canadian Engineer Monetary Times, Toronto.

Canadian Foundry Co. Toronto. plans.

Canadian National Railway, Head Office Montreal, plans, line drawings. CNR Winnipeg Regional Office, records, plans.

Canadian Northern Railway Co. *Encyclopaedia* CNR, Montreal, 1918.

Canadian Pacific Corporate Archives Montreal. photographs and line drawings.

Chesapeake and Ohio Historical Society Alderson, W. Virginia, drawing.

The Civil Engineer and Architects Journal London, England, 1859.

The Commercial, (Winnipeg) Issue 12, Dec. 1882.

Cordeal, Ernest *Railroad Operations,* Simmons-Boardman, New York, 1924.

Dewsnup, Ernest Ritson *Railway Organization and Working,* University of Chicago Press, Chicago, 1906.

Dominion Bridge Co. Lachine, "Twin Span Turntables," Montreal, 1921. numerous draughtsman's plans, line drawings.

Dorman, Robert A. *A Statutory History of the Steam and Electric Railways of Canada.* King's Printer, Ottawa, 1938.

Encyclopaedia *Britannica* 11th ed.

The Engineer London, Eng. issue 1 Feb. 1918.+

Engineering News, also under title **Engineering news-Record** Hill Publishing Co., Engineering News Publishing Co., New York.

General Electric Review issue Sept. 1926.+

Grand Trunk Railway Co. *Report of the Special Committee appointed to inquire and report as to the condition, management and prospects of the Grand Trunk Railway Co.,* John Lovell, Toronto, 1857.

Report of Thomas E. Blackwell of the Grand Trunk Railway Company of Canada for 1859, Waterlow and Sons, London, 1860.

Guinn, Rodger "An Historical Assessment of the Four Structures in the Canadian National East Yards, Winnipeg, Man." Research Bulletin No. 126, National Historic Parks and Sites Br., Parks Canada, Ottawa, 1980.

Haas, Exum A. "Modern Tendencies in Roundhouse Design," *Journal of the Western Society of Engineers,* Society of Western Engineers, Chicago, Nov. 1919.

Independent Buyers' Guide Manufacturers Products List Co., Montreal, 1911.

Kirkman, Marshall M. *the Science of Railways,* 12 Vol., Vol. 1, 3 and 7, World Railway Publishing Co., New York, 1900.

Lavallée, Omer S.A. *Van Horne's Road,* Railfare, Montreal, 1974.

Locomotive Engineering after 1900 Railway and Locomotive Engineering, New York.

Lowe, J. Norman "New Uses for Roundhouses," *Canadian Transportation,* June 1964, Southam-Maclean Publications, Toronto.
Canadian National in the East, British Railways Modelers of North America series, Vol. 1, Calgary, 1981.

Merriman, Thaddeus and Thoms H. Wiggin, ed. *American Civil Engineers' Handbook,* 5th ed., John Wiley and Sons, New York, 1938.

North Shore Railway of Canada *Specifications for Construction and Equipment of the Piles Branch,* Augustin Cote, Quebec, 1875.

Nova Scotia Railroad *Report of the Pictou Railway 1867,* Halifax, 1867.

Ontario Northlands Railway North Bay, Ontario, records and plans.

Ontario. Public Archives
Andrew Merriless Coll. RG8 Railway Sessional Papers, Toronto and Nipissing Railroad.

Quebec, Montreal, Ottawa and Occidental Railway *Report concerning the Quebec, Montreal, Ottawa and Occidental Railway, 1881.* Queen's Printer, Quebec, 1881.

Railroad and Engineering Journal New York, 1889.+

Railroad Gazette Simmons-Boardman, New York, 1873-1903.

Railway Age Simmons-Boardman, New York, 1920-8.

Railway Age Gazette Simmons-Boardman, New York, 1910-16.

Railway and Locomotive Engineering Angus Sinclair, New York, 1903-28.

Railway and Shipping World (successive titles thereafter – Railway and Marine World, Canadian Railway and Marine World, Canadian Transportation). Toronto, 1902-50.+

Railway Engineering and Maintenance New York, 1912-36.+

Railway Maintenance Engineer Chicago, New York, 1919.+

Railway Master Mechanic 1892.+

Railway Mechanical Engineer Simmons-Boardman, New York, 1919-23.

Railway Review Chicago, 1887-1921.+

Roberval and Saguenay Railroad drawing.

Temiskaming and Northern Ontario Railway *Annual Reports Temiskaming and Northern Ontario Railway Commission for years 1902-4, 1910, 1912-3, 1915, 1917,* King's Printer, Toronto.

Toronto, Hamilton and Buffalo Railway Engineer's Office, Hamilton, Ontario. Plans, drawings, specifications.

Turner, Robert D. *Railroaders Recollections from the Steam Era in B.C.,* Sound Heritage Series No. 31, B.C. Public Archives, Victoria, B.C.+

Winnipeg Daily Sun 15 Sept., 1883.

Woodworth, Marguerite *History of the Dominion Atlantic Railway,* Dominion Atlantic Railway, Kentville, N.S., 1936.

INDEX by place name

THE BOSTON MILLS PRESS